My Cyprus

JOACHIM SARTORIUS, born in 1946, is a poet, translator and commentator. He grew up in Tunis and spent twenty years in the diplomatic service in New York, Istanbul and Nicosia. He was Secretary General of the Goethe Institut until 2000, and from 2001–2011 was Director of the Berliner Festspiele. He lives and works in Berlin. A collection of his poetry, *Ice Memory* (Carcanet, 2006), is available in English.

My Cyprus

by
Joachim Sartorius

Translated by Stephen Brown

First published in English in 2014 as *The Geckos of Bellapais* by
The Armchair Traveller
4 Cinnamon Row
London SW11 3TW

First published in paperback as *My Cyprus* in 2021

www.hauspublishing.com
@HausPublishing

First published in 2013 as *Mein Zypern*
by mareverlag, Hamburg
Copyright © mareverlag, 2013

English translation copyright © Stephen Brown, 2014

Excerpt on p v from Costas Montis, *Moments*, Zavallis Press, Nicosia: 1963,
translated by Amaranth Sitas and Charles Dodd
Excerpt on p v from Galatopoulos Christodoulos in Theoklis Kouyialis (ed), *27
Centuries of Cypriot Poetry*, PEN Publications: 1983, translated by John Vickers

A CIP catalogue record for this book is available from the British Library

ISBN: 978-1-909961-78-4
Ebook ISBN: 978-1-913368-27-2

Typeset in Garamond by MacGuru Ltd

Printed in the United Kingdom

The translation of this work was supported by a grant from the Goethe Institut,
which is funded by the German Ministry of Foreign Affairs.

With what were these mountains woven together,
where were these mountains imprinted,
this sea, this sky,
how were they imprinted
that we use only them for comparison,
that we have only them for models?

COSTAS MONTIS (1914–2004)

Even from broken glasses
was I able to drink wine and I did so!

GALATOPOULOS CHRISTODOULOS (1902–1953)

For Anna and Andrea

The summer house of the last architect of the Crown

My father had a saying: 'Every man has his house'. He didn't mean anything unusual, certainly nothing metaphysical, just that every man has a house he especially loves. The house I love is on Cyprus, in Lapithos, on the north coast. I lived there for two summers and failed to buy it. In those days I rejected ownership, because it binds, it chains you to one place and then you want to move on. Later, as I discovered, a tycoon from Istanbul bought it, and I don't dare imagine what it looks like today, especially inside. I made a huge mistake, not accepting Mark Harrison's offer.

I met Mark in the middle of the 1980s at the Blue Moon Bar. The Blue Moon stood on slightly higher ground on the edge of the pretty port of Kyrenia. It was small and gloomy, but when winter was over you could sit outside on the rickety wicker stools, watching the swaying boats in the harbour through the distinctive foliage of the fig trees, ordering one rakı or gin after another. Mark was a regular there, but it was only on my fourth or fifth visit that we began to talk. He slurred a little. I guessed he was around 40, a tall, fair man leaning against the bar, but he looked tired, unhealthy, as if pickled in alcohol. He wanted to know where I'd come from.

1

'From Nicosia,' I said.

'How did you get over the border so easily,' he asked, 'if you're coming from over there?' By 'over there' he meant the Greek part of the island.

'I have a special passport,' I said, 'so I can travel back and forth.' I thought it would be pretentious to say that it was a diplomatic passport. Orhan, the bar owner, was busying himself with the glasses while listening intently.

Mark got straight to the point: 'I own a beautiful house in Lapithos. Perhaps you know the village. A couple of miles from here. I need money. I'd like to rent the house. A hundred pounds a month.'

As it was already dark, we made an appointment for the following day. Nicosia boiled in summer; the yellow heat of the Mesaoria plain gathered itself there and made life unbearable. Even after the sun had gone down, the walls radiated a tremendous heat. To swap that large oven of shadow and glare for a house by the sea for the summer seemed tempting to me. I was curious.

We met in front of the house in the middle of the afternoon. The house stood a little apart from the centre of the village, on a square bordered by three large, majestic houses. A couple of donkeys, laden and overladen with bundles of fresh mulberry branches, each load three times the size of the animal, came down the slope and trotted across the square, black with moisture.

Mark was standing in front of one of the houses. It was covered in a snow-white wash, dismissive of the outside world, with no windows in the walls on the street. He pushed the door open and we came almost immediately, after a small hallway, into a vast room, a vaulted space, a veritable refectory with a fireplace at the gable end and – save for some seating upholstered in white – rigorously bare. Three doors led out onto a terrace, which was shaded by an overhang of the building and which culminated in three gently pointed round arches on columns of yellow sandstone. The terrace and the arcade formed one side of an inner courtyard, in the style of a cloister, open on two sides and overgrown with grass and reeds. There was a goldfish pond in the centre of the square, next to a mighty pepper tree, which was just in bloom, and two mimosas. I thought spontaneously of the Garden of Eden. A further building adjoined this open quadrangle, which we reached by crossing the terrace and another, smaller yard, with a fountain in it. This building contained the bedrooms and bathrooms, with a loggia on the first storey. Mark insisted on showing me every room. He shoved the shutters open and the branches of a jacaranda tree, covered in blue flowers, reached into the room. He gestured towards the sea, which lay perhaps two miles away.

'The property extends as far as the road by the sea. It's not so well kept. A gigantic lemon grove all the way to the coast.'

We sat ourselves down at a crude wooden table under the arches on the first terrace.

'You may be wondering why the house is so empty, so bare, only white walls and the basics, tables and chairs. It wasn't always like this. My father collected a great many things: Roman busts, old books, vases, icons. The house was a little museum. But after the invasion, the Turkish soldiers took everything with them. That was 1974. Ten years ago. Heaven knows where all that stuff is now.'

Gradually I learnt that Mark was the son of the last architect for the Crown, that is to say, the last chief architect of the British colonial administration on Cyprus: Sir Austen Harrison. This was his summer house. He had come across a Greek wine cellar, built over by the Romans, on his forays through Lapithos. Harrison erected the house on these foundations in the early 1950s.

We quickly agreed a deal. Even if Mark had reconsidered and trebled the rent, I would have acceded to every demand. I was hopelessly in love with the property, from the moment I stepped out of the central hall, under the columns and into the first of the gardens, pushing the drooping branches of jasmine to one side with my hand, and sensed the house's human proportions. It was not until much later, perhaps my last summer before I left Cyprus, that I re-read Lawrence Durrell's book *Bitter Lemons* and found the following passage, which I had forgotten:

But all this was swallowed up in despair and envy when we entered Austen Harrison's house and found its romantic owner seated gravely by his own lily-pond, apparently engaged in psychoanalysing a goldfish. He was a noble personage, with his finely minted Byzantine emperor's head and the spare athletic repose of his tall figure ... He represented that forgotten world where style was not only a literary imperative but an inherent method of approaching the world of books, roses, statues and landscapes. His house was a perfect illustration of the man. He had taken over an old Cypriot wine-magazine, or perhaps stable, and converted it with a tenderness and discretion which made the whole composition sing – the long arched room lined with books, from whose recesses glowed icons; the shaded terrace with its pointed arches, the summer house, the lily-pond. All this was an illustration of philosophic principles – an illustration of how the good life might, and how it should, be lived.

I moved into the house in the summer of 1984 and spent three months there. I did the same again in the summer of 1985. Then Mark wanted to sell the house, the house that Lawrence Durrell in another part of his book called 'the most beautiful house in all of the Eastern Mediterranean'. He needed money and I didn't grab my chance. But those two summers belong among the happiest of my life.

'Splendidly fertile and famous everywhere for its lemons'

On the evening of the day we moved in, I sat on the terrace under the arches. The children, Anna and Andrea, were already asleep. We had brought only the essentials with us from Nicosia – bed linen, towels, flip-flops, a few books, swimming goggles. That afternoon, after our arrival, we had been shopping in Lapithos. The *bakkal* had everything: fragrant bread, salad, vegetables, coffee, cardamom, the Turks' beloved *pastirma*, a strongly spiced cured beef, as well as candles, honey-soaked *baklava*, and a carton of 'Lal', a rosé wine from the Turkish mainland, whose fresh, cool edge I prized, especially on hot summer days.

We had taken possession of the house cautiously. We allocated the bedrooms. I placed a watercolour by Niki Marangou, a good friend from Nicosia, on the mantelpiece. We stowed our shopping in the kitchen. Measured against the generous proportions of the other rooms, the kitchen was astonishingly small and fitted out with only the barest necessities. Under the plates of pale green pressed glass, I found a larger, painted ceramic dish, which – it soon became apparent – was the only item in the house with a direct connection to its architect. I own this plate to this day. It measures 35 centimetres in diameter. Its broad black border is interrupted above and below by lettering. Above, in black capital letters, stand the words: 'AUSTEN HARRISON'; and below: 'LAPITHOS'. A tall, slender figure, undoubtedly Sir Austen himself, occupies the vertical axis of the white centre of the plate. The figure wears long, baggy white trousers and a white tunic, and its yellow-brown fox-like face is crowned with a shock of wildly dishevelled hair. It is carrying a broad folding ruler, the emblem of the architect. The whole is carelessly sketched, very playful. The architect prances, a bright, light, captivating figure. Along with some photographs, this plate is my strongest bond to that house. I would love to know whether Austen himself drew the sketch or – more likely – it was the work of a gifted friend. I have to do some research in the archives of the British colonial ministry, dig out some drawings by Sir Austen and make a comparison.

On our first evening I straightaway piled grapes and figs on that plate and set it down on the wooden table under the arcade. I fetched a wobbly standard lamp out of the hall and sat down at the table where a couple of days earlier I had signed my tenancy agreement with Mark. The sky had lost almost all colour. Only the little pond retained a remnant of blue. Bats darted back and forth between the pointed arches. Two geckos promenaded up the stone wall, light grey, almost translucent, with black button eyes, on the hunt for insects. In the cone of light thrown on the ground by the lamp, I saw a dried-out, whitish trail of slime next to my toes, a dented circle made by a slug, which was by now next to the stone pillar, being cut to pieces by large red ants. I felt that I was a part of this world of small animals, the geckos, ants, spiders, nightjars and bats, or rather, that I had been subsumed into the mass of nature which surrounded the house. No wind stirred, but the pepper tree swayed from side to side. A dark green fragrance carried over from the lemon grove and mingled with the cloying scent of jasmine. When I stood in front of the round arches, I saw the pitch-black, jagged face of the Kyrenia Mountains behind the pallid house. In that moment, the Lal tasted of cold shadow, of a deliciously cool shadow. The light of the moon emerged from behind the trees. It was so bright that the decorative grooves on the capital of the column cast a sharp shadow in front of me. It made me think of the curled ear of a Greek goddess. One of the two geckos disappeared into it.

I had brought a few books about Cyprus with me from the small library at the embassy, as well as reprints of old travel books. Now that I was a resident of Lapithos, I wanted to find out everything about this village, my summer residence near to the capital Nicosia, my second home.

British travel writers from the beginning of the last century are unanimous in calling Lapithos the most beautiful village on the entire island. Surrounded by orange and lemon groves, it is constantly watered by springs that rise in the nearby mountains. Some authors claim that it was first settled by the Spartans under Praxander, others believe that the Phoenicians from Tyre on the Lebanese coast founded a city here. In the diary of the Italian Thomaso Porcacchi, who published his book *L'Isole piu famose del mondo* in Venice in 1572, I found the following entry: 'Lapethos, sited two miles from Cerines [presumably what is now Kyrenia], was also once a capital city. Its last king was Pisistratus, a companion of Alexander the Great. Now it is a small village of the same name, splendidly fertile and famous everywhere for its lemons.' Ah Porcacchi! Across four hundred years I raise my glass to you!

Rupert Gunnis writes in the greatest detail about ancient Lapithos in his book *Historic Cyprus*, published in London in 1936. Gunnis's guidebook describes the ruins, castles, monasteries, cities and villages of Cyprus with a meticulousness bordering on hysteria, creating for the reader the image of an island entirely coated in churches, remains and ruins. In the section on Lapithos, Gunnis describes first of all the five churches in and around the village, all of more recent date and, according to Gunnis, uninteresting. No doubt they are now in a still more lamentable state, having been pillaged by the Turkish soldiers in 1974. Gunnis's focus is fixed on the ruins of Lambousa, right by the sea to the west of Lapithos. This ancient city, founded in the 8th century before Christ, achieved power and influence in Roman and Byzantine times and was famous for its amphorae and ephebes. Now, Gunnis tells us, only a few blocks of cut stone, some half-destroyed mosaic floors and the remnants of a lighthouse are left. Plundered by the Arabs in the 7th century, the city returned to prominence in the early Middle Ages under Crusader rule. Two buildings survive from this time: the church of Saint Evlavios and the Acheiropoietos Monastery, which is to say 'built without hands', on account of the legend that the Virgin Mary transported the entire monastery over the sea from Anatolia, where it was in danger of being destroyed. Its oldest elements, notably its cruciform church, date back to the 13th century. Gunnis conjectures that the marble columns in the side chapels are older still, originating from the Byzantine period. He praises the Corinthian capitals, the elaborate floors of many-coloured marble and the grave slab of a Venetian, one Alessandro Flatros, who financed the enlargement of the apse aisle. Between this church and the church of Saint Evlavios, in the middle of what was once a quarry, stands a chapel entirely hewn from the rock, dedicated to Saint Evlambios. A unique trove of early 7th-century silver was found here in the early 1900s. John Pierpont Morgan bought a part of it, which is now exhibited at the Metropolitan Museum in New York. The rest was divided between the Archaeological Museum in Nicosia and the British Museum in London. The objects in London – amongst others, an elaborately worked silver plate bearing an image of the god Bacchus and a serving spoon whose bowl shows a ram, embossed in exquisitely fine detail – bear witness to the ingenuity and splendid, refined lifestyle of Lambousa's Byzantine inhabitants.

I snapped the book shut, tired and happy. Who could believe, I said to myself, that a pocket-book compendium could fit in so much archaeology? And it was not just about the ruins and the archaeology. Beyond the facts and figures, it was about nothing less than world history as island history. I was tired, yes, but I was electrified. Even here in Lapithos and its ancient precursor Lambousa, between the sea and the Kyrenia mountain range, the entire history of Cyprus was gathered as if under a magnifying glass. The Phoenicians had landed here and the Ptolemies had replaced them. The Byzantine period followed the Roman. After the Crusaders, after the Kingdom of the Lusignans and their romantic castles, came the Venetian occupation, until in 1571 the Ottoman Empire annexed the island. The complex of the monastery and churches at Lambousa fascinated me especially. I had promised the children that the following day we would explore the beaches to the east of Kyrenia. But Lambousa was next on my agenda after that. Suddenly it occurred to me that Mark, during one of our meetings at the Blue Moon Bar, when we were speaking about the all-too-forceful presence of the Turkish military here in the North, had said that the oldest, most beautiful part of the coast here was a restricted area. The Turks had turned a monastery into a military academy. Had he meant Lambousa? I emptied my glass of Lal and saw myself striding unfazed past the warning signs and the marauding bands of grim-faced Turkish soldiers and onwards, to the domes of Lambousa.

I turned out the lamp, went to my room and fell asleep, near to my sea.

'The birds are here!
The snails are here!'

A few days before our little move to Lapithos, Niki Marangou threw a party at her house in Nicosia. The long summer break stood before us. The schools had just closed their doors. Soon the Nicosians would scatter in all directions, to the coast at Limassol, Paphos or Akamas, or, if well heeled, to Athens, London or Paris. It was a small, merry gathering: the ever-cheerful, eccentric, mustachioed mayor Lellos Demetriades, the choreographer and dancer Arianna Economou with her German husband, the painter Horst Weierstall, the gallery-owner Gloria Kassianides and the head of the Antiquities Authority Vassos Karageorghis, a stiff character, God's anointed propagandist for Hellenism but ferociously well informed. We were joined later by George Lanitis, a journalist who fancied himself a great photographer and took flashy pictures of unbearably red poppy fields, gnarled olive trees and hazy blue beaches. Two years before the invasion, he had built a property on a hill by Bellapais with a spectacular view of the whole northern coastline, and he could not get over having lost it all.

As always at such gatherings in Nicosia, our conversation turned straightaway to politics. It was unavoidable, a kind of law of nature, and ultimately paralysing. The United Nations had put forward a new peace plan, based on a federation of the two parts of the country and, as always, the

Greek Cypriots, including the majority of the liberal souls gathered there that night, had rejected the suggestion in disgust. I dared not say a word about the house I had rented in the North, where I intended to spend the summer. Unlike me, the employee of an embassy and so 'responsible' for both parts of the island, they could not travel there and would not be able to visit me. In those days Cyprus's internal border was impermeable, wickeder and more inhumane even than the German partition had ever been.

'The Turks are a glacier, relentlessly pushing everything forward,' proclaimed Lanitis in a warning tone, mixing up his climates.

I was reminded of a remark by a German ambassador in Ankara, who had compared Turkey to a powerful bull in a lush pasture. The Greek threats and loutish behaviour were mosquito bites. The bull might swish his tail or roll over onto his other side, but nothing more. Lellos Demetriades, inspired by the West German 'policy of small steps', told us about a meeting he had just had with the mayor of the Turkish part of Nicosia. They had agreed to embark upon joint projects in the No Man's Land near to the 'green line' and to try at least to gather together architects and town planners to consider the future of a sometime reunified city.

All had their sad stories of the Turkish occupation of the North. Niki, our graceful hostess, told the story of her uncle, who had taken over his father's timber business in Famagusta, married a Greek woman from Port Said in Egypt and had built one of the very first stately villas right on the beach at Famagusta – 'with a vast terrace and white colonnades running down to the sea'. The estate of a Greek Great Gatsby rose before our eyes. This Mitsos had been a book fanatic, a bibliophile who had, Niki said, built a collection of all the travel literature in the world, though most especially accounts of journeys in the Holy Land and the Levant and to Cyprus. The library in the villa was panelled in oak. Curtains of heavy orange silk filtered the light. As a young girl she had often sought refuge there, found volumes of poetry and copied out the poems and changed them, made them her own. Later her uncle had given her a first edition of the poems of Constantine Cavafy, published in Alexandria in 1935. It was the only book from that library to have survived.

'We were never able to discover anything about the fate of the pictures and the books,' Niki said. 'The only thing that's certain is that the entire area has been cordoned off and uninhabited since 1974.'

I pictured a veranda completely overrun by plants and books covered with a layer of fine sand.

I had been in my post in Nicosia for eight months by then, and I had heard stories like this almost every day, every evening. I had great sympathy with the Greek Cypriots' traumas and sense of loss. You might have thought that in the ten years since the Turkish invasion time would have healed or soothed their wounds a little. But the fatal problem was that the Greeks in Nicosia, standing in their houses, on their balconies, looked to the north and saw the Pentadaktylos, the five jags of mountain behind which Kyrenia and all their possessions lay. Day after day memory offered them no escape.

And yet I failed to see that this cruel division was

14

exclusively the fault of the Turks, or of the last colonial power, the British. Almost exactly 30 years earlier, in 1954, Georgios Grivas, a crazed retired colonel of the Greek army and Cypriot native, had landed in a secluded cove at Akamas in order to begin a guerilla war against the British and to force the island to unite with the mother country, Greece. His rigid Panhellenism found a terrific sounding board in the peculiar constitution of Cyprus, namely the millennium-long hegemony of the Orthodox Church. Its bishop had ranked alongside the Patriarchs of Constantinople, Alexandria and Antioch from the 5th century. Even under the Ottomans, from 1571, he had remained the undisputed ruler of the entire Greek community on the island. In 1950, when Michael Mouskos, later to be Archbishop Makarios III, held a plebiscite in every church in Cyprus, the result left the people's will in little doubt: 96 per cent of Greek Cypriots – who constituted 80 per cent of the island's population – voted for *enosis*, union with the motherland.

I didn't dare point out to my friends that this vehement Panhellenism had driven the Turkish minority into a corner and explained much of the stubborn attitude which the Turkish Cypriots had displayed since independence in 1960 under their leader Rauf Denktaş. They were simply nervous. They felt on the brink of being besieged. I also didn't dare to ask whether this revolt against Great Britain, led by a pistolero and a prelate, had not carried within it the germ of the later poison.

Now our little group was once again cursing the British colonial administration. Here they were in the right. It was the British government that had at the very beginning encouraged Ankara to gamble with Cyprus, and when the junta had taken power in Athens, it was the British who in July 1974 had replaced the volatile Archbishop Makarios with the hitman Nikos Sampson. When Bülent Ecevit, then the Turkish premier, had demanded in London that Prime Minister Harold Wilson and Foreign Secretary James Callaghan take joint action with the Turks, London had refused to so much as lift a finger. The following day the Turks began preparing to land on Cyprus. The Turkish armed forces seized a beachhead near Kyrenia and dropped paratroopers further inland. For several weeks there was a ceasefire. The Turks made it clear that they no longer considered themselves bound by earlier treaties and wanted an immediate partition of the island.

'Surely London had to do something!' cried Lanitis. 'They had military bases on the island. They had a strong air force. But they did nothing! Why?' He fixed his gaze on me, brandishing his glass of red wine wildly, as if I were Harold Wilson in the flesh.

'I don't know, George,' I said. 'If in doubt, London was always for Turkey and against Athens. And perhaps the British were weary of Makarios, who had been hastily reinstated and for them was little better than a Fidel Castro in a cassock.'

'I simply don't understand it,' said Lanitis, suddenly distressed. 'Makarios had charisma. He was subtle. He had dignity.'

'I never had personal experience of him,' I said. 'But he fascinates me. An archbishop who more than anything else played the role of a Third-World leader. When had that happened before? He met with Tito, with Nehru, with Nasser. He was the absolute opposite of the restored Athenian government. And at the same time completely contradicted what the former colonial power expected of him. London's sluggishness after the invasion was the British revenge.'

'That was when the real catastrophe happened,' pontificated Vassos Karageorghis.

In fact, weeks after the landing, during a deceptive calm, the Turks launched a second surge and in less than 72 hours had occupied two-fifths of the island, pushing their troops forward to the so-called Attila Line, which ran from Morphou Bay above Nicosia to Famagusta. With occupation came ethnic cleansing. Almost a third of the Greek population – around 180,000 people – were driven from house and home and hounded southwards over the Attila Line. In the other direction around 50,000 Turkish islanders set off into the north, partly out of fear, partly under pressure from the Turkish regime installed there, which needed to strengthen its demographics and had committed itself to a complete separation of the two ethnic groups. This separation was felt especially strongly in Nicosia, carved in two by barricades, sandbags and barbed wire.

'Enough politics!' cried Niki. 'The solution is a long way off!' She brought a roast lamb out of the kitchen, together with an aubergine bake and stewed tomatoes, everything enveloped in a cloud of garlic. Now the conversation took a different turn. Karageorghis reported on the latest excavations near Kourion. The archaeologists had found mosaics to rival the Dionysus mosaics in Nea Paphos, as well as numerous tablets which would help to illuminate the cult of Aphrodite in late antiquity.

'Ah,' I sighed. 'I would so like to have one white marble shoulder! Wouldn't have to be Aphrodite. Any goddess would be enough for me.'

Niki told the story of a man who, many years ago, had dealt antiques in Koshi, on an arterial road out of Nicosia. He had specialised in fragments of statues. Farmers used to bring him so many pieces that he didn't know what to do except store them, so he had one room of his house dedicated to toes, feet and knees, another for arms and hands, and a third for shoulders and heads. Later the man came to fancy himself an artist. He had assembled the ancient parts and filled in the missing bits with plaster, which he modelled himself. He sold the results alongside goat's cheese and green asparagus. Well-intentioned customers had pointed out to him that he really ought to make statues himself without relying on the old fragments. I discovered to my regret that this shop no longer existed and the would-be artist – nicknamed the 'Polybius of Marble' – had died a few years earlier.

Karageorghis turned his attention to me: 'Listen! A crazy amount of stuff is found on this island. In practically every field, under every hill. In my museum we have a heap of duplicates. Tear jugs, vases, oil lamps, clay statues and so on. We sell the duplicates, because we simply don't have enough storage space. Come round and see!'

'Even a shoulder of white marble? Or a breast?' I asked.

'No. Not that. But you will find something that will make you happy.'

'Your conversation reminds me of my nanny,' interjected Niki. 'She was Turkish, buxom, with spherical breasts. She sometimes let me play with them. We were living then in Limassol. She was in love with a policeman who worked as a security guard at the old castle. It was a museum in those days. One time she took me with her to the museum and the policeman led us round, explaining all the ancient objects as best he could. My nanny had never been in a museum before. After each explanation from the policeman she prostrated herself in front of the display case and cried out "Allah! Allah! To think I might have died without seeing this!"'

'Do you know what became of her?' asked Arianna.

'Grivas's men shot her in the sixties.'

Gloria Kassianides talked about Greek refugees from Karpas, the spit of land east of Famagusta. They would phone her up and let her know: 'The snails are here!' And in autumn they would phone her: 'The mushrooms are here!' or 'The birds are here!' even though in Nicosia there were no snails and no mushrooms and next to no birds.

'Old habits,' said Gloria. 'On the Karpas peninsula the birds came in the autumn. The men would take their bottle of brandy and their rifles and stay in the fields for three days and shoot all the birds dead. This rhythm is in them and it will never leave them, no matter where they are.'

So all conversations return imperceptibly to the island's troubled situation. How could they do otherwise?

I asked Niki about her painting. Looking at her, vivacious and at the same time with a wonderful Levantine ease, you saw nothing of the turbulent life she had already lived – she was by then 36 years old. When she graduated from school in Cyprus she decided to escape all the limits of the island and went to Berlin to study sociology. This was in the wild late sixties. When she came back to the island five years later and straightaway drank a rum with mint on the harbour at Kyrenia and let her eyes soak up the Mediterranean, she found she could no longer understand the demonstrations, revolutionary machinations and dogged left-wingers of West Berlin and tossed her leftist socialisation into the sea. She took up the study of icon painting and began to write poems and novels. More recently she had made collages and painted watercolours, which she now, at my request, showed us.

A fat yellow grasshopper on the white balustrade of a balcony. Seascapes thick with blues and greens. Colourful street scenes, which she had brought back with her from Alexandria, where she had won the Cavafy Prize for her poems. I liked the delicate yet confident lines of these pages, as well as their rich colouring. The colours were the colours of the island in spring and in the early days of summer. On a previous visit I had bought a collage showing the Gate of the Sun and the Gate of the Moon in ancient Alexandria, inspired by a poem by George Seferis. As we looked through the new pictures, I decided that I would take that collage with me to Lapithos.

We emptied a final glass and paid our compliments to Niki's multifarious arts. Then our little group dispersed. I went home on foot. Some bars were still open. Music blared out of an old jukebox, which must have spent its better days in England. There were men lined up along the counter, and bottles lined up above them, with a few family photos and a portrait of an archbishop in full regalia – Makarios most likely. As I walked past, the last open shop, a fruit stall, let down its steel shutters, making a great din. Political slogans were sprayed all over them: I could make out 'ENOSIS' and 'CLERIDES STEP DOWN!'

For a short distance I followed the line of the Venetian city wall, which enclosed the old city in the shape of a jagged star, then went past Vassos Karageorghis's museum to our house on Gladstonos Street, calm and fringed with many old palm trees. Nicosia was a friendly little provincial city, and I often asked myself why I had not really been able to make friends with it. The city desired transience, a desire intensified in the summer, being so far from the sea. Perhaps that was it, along with the wounds of partition, which the enterprising Greeks, busy as bees, knew how to cover up, until the moment when you were in the old city and the multitude of empty, half-destroyed buildings with their pockmarked façades suddenly loomed in front of you and made you feel the tension generated by the city's split.

The Moon Beach

'What are we doing today?' asked Andrea, her eyes sparkling. We were having breakfast out on the terrace under the arcade, in that playful mood a new, as yet unfamiliar environment will give you.

I had woken very early and, leaving the house behind me, wandered into the lemon groves. Between the trees I saw the coastline sprinkled with points of orange light. The sea lay noiseless and unmoving in the June morning. Everything seemed to want to catch its breath again before the fierce heat. I caught my breath too and with that breath a feeling of contentment rose inside me. Life, which in Nicosia had seemed to pass me by in diplomatic circles, official meetings and small errands, was here for the grasping. It had entered into an alliance with Nature, and I made a wish that it would not so quickly release me again.

'Today we're looking for the Moon Beach,' I said. 'Beyond Kyrenia.'

'Moon Beach?' Andrea raised her curved, blonde, almost invisible eyebrows.

'It's Mark's name for a particular bay. It should be deserted. With a broad curve, exactly the shape of a crescent moon. And if we're lucky, we'll see some giant turtles.'

Anna and Andrea drummed their small fists on the table with excitement.

We took the car and drove past Kyrenia, past Bellapais up above it, and then shortly after the village of Kazaphani turned off onto a gravel track, which seemed to lead down to the coast. For me a clear message lay waiting in the hundred details of this short journey: the castle at Kyrenia, the mighty gothic abbey at Bellapais, the Crusader castles of Saint Hilarion and Buffavento, set on the blue-green mountain ridge like great feats of imagination, were heralds of a glittering gothic Middle Ages, a kind of early Mediterranean Romanticism, which had never lost its radiance and counted all that had happened since as nothing.

After a couple of hundred metres our gravel track simply ended in sand. There was vegetation all around us, bushes covered in white thorns with eucalyptus trees rising over them. Further away in the maquis were the red splashes of scattered oleander bushes, which seemed to be unfurling themselves with the rising sun. A thick pink light, becoming liquid. With our picnic basket, sunshade and towels, we trudged off across the fiercely hot sand, towards where we judged the sea to be. The children moaned because the glowing sand was trickling into their open sandals.

'We'll be there in no time,' I declared. 'Wimping out is not allowed.'

Then suddenly the land was sloping away from us. We had only to clamber up a small dune which stood in our way. From the top of it we looked out onto the vast, deserted bay lying before us.

'All to ourselves!' shouted Andrea.

We stumbled and tripped and tumbled down the long slope. The sea was a long way below the dunes and stretched itself out unhindered in every shade of blue. We dropped all our things at the edge of the surf, pulled our clothes off and simply kept on going until the smoothness and cool of the water completely surrounded us. We swam, we paddled, we dived, we played dead.

'Your eyelashes moved!' shouted Anna and splashed me with water. We let ourselves drift, engulfed in particles of light, our faces caressed by a warm gentle wind. At that moment we wanted nothing else in the world.

Later we ran right around the broad curve, looking for mussels, crab claws and starfish. Anna found a mask of some rubbery material already eroded by the salty water, with a broad, grinning face and a striped yellow and black hair-style. She insisted that this was the face of Maya the Bee. The children fooled around, pulling faces and practising handstands on the sand. Of giant turtles there was no trace, but at the end of the bay, between two rocks, we discovered a washed-up swordfish with thin, malignant jaws. A demon, without doubt, dressed in a blue-slate skin. Tough, invincible, even in death.

The disc of the sun was blazing in the sky. We clustered together in our umbrella's small circle of shade, back pressed against back, while the sea changed colour: blue, blue-green, green-blue, deep blue – a blue so dark the only other place I've seen it is a Seljuk tile. The goat's cheese tasted delicious with fresh white bread, olives and honey. We had strawberries – *Erdbeeren* – for dessert.

'When do you get earthquakes – *Erdbeben*?' asked Andrea.

'An *Erdbeben* happens when the *Erdbeeren* are ripe,' joked Anna.

The conversation turned to dream jobs.

'Spot painter on ladybirds?' wondered Anna.

'Pupil roller for peacock butterflies?'

'Horn player in a band of buffalo?'

We agreed in the end on sea-urchin-spine-puller.

Much later, after one more bout of swimming, we trudged wearily back to the car and treated ourselves on the journey home to a stop in Kyrenia, at a café right on the harbour, in arm's reach of the moored boats. Still dazed by too much light, sun and salt, we sipped our ice-cold lemonades out of tall glasses and made the long spoons tinkle on the glass. A figure emerged out of the violet shadows of the fortress. It was Ahmet, the fisherman. He was well-known locally for his stories. He sat himself down at our table without ceremony and lived up to his reputation: 'Do you want to hear the peculiar story of what happened to me last week? Well,' said Ahmet, without waiting a moment for us to respond, 'I saw a fat seagull, which had caught a squid and was carrying it in its beak. I snatched the squid off the seagull and then used it as bait on my fishing line. Because with a squid you catch big fish. But no fish bit. Not even a small one. Well, OK, I thought to myself, I'll take the calamari back with me to my house and cook it up for myself. But when I threw the squid into the frying pan, the seething oil splashed right up – and one drop hit my right eye. It hissed. I had hellish pains for four whole days. I thought to myself, that must be the seagull's curse. He gave me such a vicious look when I tore the squid out of his beak.'

We laughed, gloating a little.

'I can't see anything in your eye,' said Anna. I stood Ahmet a double rakı.

On our return to Lapithos I found a small gecko in the kitchen, on the rack over the stove. He was fearless and, it seemed to me, looking at me reproachfully. You've interrupted me on the hunt for flies and millipedes and winged termites, he seemed to say. It was only later, when we were living in Bellapais, that I came to understand that these lizards want to talk to us, in their own manner, to signal to us with their broad toes, a kind of elegant tremor in answer to our chatter, and that they change their colour when something does not please them.

For the next two days Anna and Andrea painted only animals in their notebooks: starfish, mussels, crabs, squid and very menacing swordfish, dropping out of palm trees onto swimmers below.

Henna and golden-yellow coins

A mere half-millennium ago, the Mediterranean was Venetian. Just wander once through the Arsenal in Venice, truly appreciate its mighty dimensions, and you will realise that the Doges' galleys and galleasses, which were once built in that shipyard, were rulers of this sea. The Venetians gave us the most beautiful cities in this part of the world: Hvar, Korčula, Dubrovnik, Rhodes, Kyrenia, Famagusta – even, with some reservations, Nicosia, with its well-preserved fortifications, which encompass the old city like an auburn poinsettia. Even in peaceable little Kyrenia, as I stood facing its powerful castle, which closes off the harbour on one side and reminded me of the tall, brutish walls of the Arsenal, I was aware of the unfettered power of *La Serenissima*. I reminded myself that the Venetians had long nurtured dreams of being a great power. As far back as 828, they stole from the Egyptians the relics of the Evangelist Mark, who was tortured to death near Alexandria, in order to give him a final resting place in Venice. The real expansion, however – Venice's triumphal march – only began hundreds of years later. The Venetians were, in essence, late descendants of the Phoenicians: they had the same dominance of the sea and the same lust for power, driven by trade.

But if you take that view of things, I said to myself, aren't you erasing more than three hundred years of Crusader rule on Cyprus, before the Venetians took control? And aren't you forgetting the Ottoman era, after Venice had gone? True enough, I said, continuing my inner dialogue, but then, if we start with the Ottomans, what did they actually do? Put a few minarets on the towers of the Gothic cathedrals in Nicosia and Famagusta. With the Crusaders, the Lusignan dynasty, the situation is completely different. In retrospect, their rule was not only the longest but also the most dazzling period in Cyprus's history. Look at it properly and you can see that the Venetians merely took over the structures that the Lusignans built, making the walls even thicker, adding still more decoration to the churches, modernising the harbours and completing the road network from a military perspective.

Thus I worked myself up over an *orta kahve* on the harbour at Kyrenia. My endeavour for the morning, to visit ancient Lambousa and its monastery, had been a wretched failure. The entire coastal area to the west of Lapithos was in effect sealed off. My conversations with the soldiers guarding all the access points from the coastal road had come to nothing. They spoke no English and my Turkish was worse than rudimentary. These simple conscripts seemed to be under the strictest instructions not to let anyone through who was not a member of the Turkish army or else called Rauf Denktaş – certainly not a sunburnt foreigner in baggy jeans and with a camera. I was not even granted a distant glimpse of the two churches and the monastery complex. Cypress and eucalyptus trees and tall bushes formed a green wall, which only strengthened my desire to penetrate the area.

In my frustration I drove to Nicosia. When you are living in two houses, as I was that summer, it goes without saying that the things you need straightaway are often at the other place and not where you at present happen to be. I had forgotten my good road map, a dictionary, the English-language editions of the poems of Costas Montis and George Seferis, and I wanted to check my post. The house at 7B Gladstonos Street lay yellow and forsaken under the palms. In spite of the closed shutters, the summer heat had built up fiercely inside. The first thing I did was to open one particular letter. A leisurely, hard-to-read scrawl, which I knew well, marauded over the envelope. Will she come? And when? I'm sorry, she wrote, I am coming, but not until the beginning of July.

I drove back in high spirits. In high spirits the Greek soldiers and the UN soldiers and the Turkish soldiers, every one of whom knew me by now, waved me through the border barriers. It seemed as if my lungs or my heart had widened. I warbled along to some kitschy Greek song, ringing out of the car radio. Suddenly life was sharpened, musical.

In Lapithos I went to pick up the children from our neighbours, who had a daughter of the same age. The father of the family, Ferit, was a civil servant, working for the local provincial government. It was early afternoon, so we decided that we would all walk together into the village, lured by chanting and the noise of a substantial crowd. On the village square, dead in the centre of it, stood a large bed. It was covered in white sheets bordered with silver. Brass posts gleamed at all four corners. A young boy, perhaps six years old, lay on a mountain of white cushions, dressed in ceremonial robes like a small sultan or a midget admiral. I have returned to this scene so often in my mind that I can to this day see it before me in every detail. The sultan costume included a white bow tie, a silver sceptre and an elaborately embroidered cape, with gold coins sewn onto it, which – Ferit told me later – were to ward off the evil eye. The small, pale sultan's white trousers had knife-sharp creases; his patent leather shoes were dusted with silver lamé.

Ferit, whose English was excellent, explained to me that the Koran itself doesn't require circumcision. But it is part of the Sunnah, the texts which set down how Muslims should behave, following how the Prophet himself lived. The ceremony has been performed for centuries and marks the entry into manhood, no matter that the boy may be extremely young. In the past, when the son of a real sultan was circumcised, the citizens of Istanbul would often have celebrated and danced for weeks at a time.

Here, the boy's vast family stood around the bed, singing and clapping, trying to bolster his courage, as he sat there under the blue sky on the four-poster bed, looking proud and miserable all at once.

'Is he hurting?' asked Anna.

'They give him a local anaesthetic,' said Ferit under his breath. 'The wound will already have begun to heal.'

Then the women crowded around the bed and painted the boy's hands with henna until they were entirely red. Other women and men threw banknotes onto the bed, as well as many small golden-yellow coins, as a further defence

30

against the evil eye. Finally a bearded man in a turban, a kind of prayer leader, sang: '*Allahu akbar! Allahu akbar!*' It is finished. He is a man. The women in their wildly patterned festive clothes stood in a semicircle around this small, frightened man. They were all of small stature, with pale, intense faces and strong chins. At the cry of the imam they were transformed for a moment into joyous Furies, throwing their arms into the air and moving their lean hips in a kind of sacred belly dance. *Allahu akbar!*

The spectacle maintained its hold over us for the entire day. The cheap white satin of the sheets glinted still in the sun, long after the sun had set.

'Why did that poor little boy have to lie on that massive bed in the sun?' asked Anna. 'It can't be any fun having everyone gawking at you!'

'How old was he?'

'A year older than you, I'd guess. Six?'

'Poor thing! I'm glad –' Andrea interrupted herself to let out a sigh, '– that we don't have willies.'

'And why did they put all that red on his hands?'

'That's called henna,' Ferit explained. 'It's a dye from a plant. It's supposed to bring good luck and joy. The women here use it to dye their hair red. Do you want to try it?'

The grammar of decoration: Bellapais

We felt so comfortable in the 'Harrison House', as the villagers called it, that we had still barely left the shady garden under the curved arches, the loggia, the pond with its goldfish. I drove to the embassy in Nicosia a few times to check that everything was in order. Twice we had made excursions to the 'Moon Beach', swum to excess, and returned to our cool, white vaults, exhausted by the fierce summery shimmering of the coast. In the evenings the wind from the mountains became trapped in our cloister. The birds broke free from their torpor and scattered leaves onto the children. I counted the bats. When I turned on the lights, the two geckos were waiting on the wall to negotiate with me.

It could have gone on like this forever. But then one soft, blue morning we decided to visit Bellapais. Lawrence Durrell had set himself up there in the 1950s. Large parts of his Cyprus book *Bitter Lemons* came into being there. I remember well the passage in which he praises the art of living as the greatest of all the arts of Bellapais. More precisely: the art of idleness. It came back to me as we encountered the villagers on our way to the Abbey. They shuffled cheerfully about, having a chitchat here, a chitchat there. A nattering, clattering queue stood in front of the aromatic bakery. Only the hair salon was empty. Two barbers sat in the shop on dark red plastic chairs and waited. One was combing his own hair. For a moment I was tempted to go inside and demand a short back and sides under the photo of Atatürk. All over the world simple barbershops have held an allure for me. In Havana, for one dollar, I had rosy red pomade massaged into my hair. In Lagos a jolly artist of coiffure wanted passionately to twirl the hair on the back of my head into three bunches. In Seoul the barber offered me a girl on the side; she was in the next room. And here, what would happen to me here? But Anna and Andrea dragged me on to the café at the entrance to the monastery.

Here the famous 'Tree of Idleness' gave shade to a few wobbly little tables and chairs. We ordered sweet mint tea. Beyond the entrance, beyond a wave of roses, oleanders and geraniums, the golden brown stone ruins of the Abbey jutted into the flawless sky. It was good for us to sip our tea in small mouthfuls, to tame our impatience a little. An old man sat at the next table, a solitary, hard, dark brown knot of a man, his right hand resting on a stick, the fingers of his left hand ceaselessly shoving along the green beads of his *tespih*, the Muslim prayer beads. A quiet *klack-klack*. As he came to the end of the beads, he swung the entire chain three or four times through the air, then began again, pushing the beads along, one bead after another. *Klack-klack*. He looked at us, leant his stick against the edge of the table, rummaged around with his right hand in his much too roomy jacket and, fishing a leaflet from out of the inside pocket, presented it to me with a crooked smile. '*Çok teşekkür ederim*,' I said. Thank you very much.

We went through the entrance gate, suddenly enveloped

in the scent of flowers, and walked at first past the cloister to the edge of the mountainside on which the Abbey sat enthroned. From there the view dropped away a hundred metres over the citrus tree plantations to the coast and its many spits of land. With this expanse still in our eyes, the arches of the cloister opened up around us in a harmonious order, emphasised still further by the four old, very slender, almost black cypresses in the centre of the square inner courtyard. Remnants of the tracery clung to some of the arches, so that I could, with a little imagination, restore the grammar of their once magnificent decorations. In the old man's leaflet I read that the Premonstratensian Order had founded the monastery in the 13th century. Bellapais Abbey, noted the author, not without pride, was the most significant Gothic building on the island.

The refectory, into which we now stepped, proved him right. The high groin vaults supported by 14 columns beckoned us into such an overwhelming stillness that the original name, *Abbaye de la Paix*, seemed the most accurate description of what this architecture sought to express. Inner peace. Six windows had been let into the north wall. Each one framed the distant blue sea. A stone pulpit, where a monk would have read out from the Holy Scriptures during mealtimes, obtained its light from a narrow opening in the ceiling vault. The refectory was naked, empty, full of strict secrets. The proportions of the stone spoke on their own, as they did in the church, which was also stripped of all decoration, and in the dormitory. I liked one room especially: the chapter house. In the middle of this four-cornered room, whose ceiling had fallen in, rose up a solitary, mighty and yet elegant marble column, which had in the past supported all the ribs of the vaulting. The children were enchanted by the stone carving of the corbels, out of which the ribs grew. They spotted a man doing battle with two mythical beasts, sirens with long, seductive hair, and an ape and a cat peering out of a pear tree.

After our tour we sat ourselves down on a wall in the cloister, overwhelmed by everything around us. I thought how calming, consoling even, it must have been for Lawrence Durrell to sit in his house in Bellapais, to write, to welcome friends and feed them, and all the time know that, just down the hill and around the corner, the Abbey was waiting for him, still, in spite of decay, in spite of the ravages of weather and man, an emblem of beauty, of radiant scale, of life happily integrated into nature. All around us the walls glowed honey-yellow in the midday sun. How had the stones come to have this particular colour? Had they stored it inside themselves, the light they had been soaking up for centuries? Hard honeycomb of ancient, yellow light?

That evening, after the children had gone to sleep, the Abbey would still not let me go. I read in Rupert Gunnis's *Historic Cyprus* how the white monks of Bellapais had not always been paragons of virtue. Their great supporter and protector had been the Lusignan king, Hugh III, who had reigned for 17 years up until the year 1284. He had allowed the monastery to expand and fitted out the Abbot with a sword, golden spurs and a bishop's cowl. According to Gunnis, it was during Hugh's reign that the buildings had achieved the form we see today. Those coats of arms that

35

we noticed during our visit over the entrance to the refectory must have been the familial devices of the Lusignans. Gunnis also points out that though this Hugh died in Tyre, he was interred with great pomp here in the church at Bellapais. It was only at the end of the Venetian period, long after the Lusignans, that the monastery's decline began. To the horror of the Provveditore in Famagusta, the monks had taken wives, sometimes several, and would select only their own children as novices. 'It is a great evil,' wrote the Provveditore to the Senate in Venice, 'that such a great abbey, such a wonder of the builder's art, should have fallen into corruption.' When the Turks conquered Cyprus in 1570 they looted the monastery, and with that the Latin, Roman-Catholic epoch on Cyprus ended forever.

As I was reading, ants had laid out a two-lane motorway under the table and between my feet into the garden. These exuberant red columns were transporting some substantial object. I turned the lamp so that its cone of light fell onto their feverish multitudes, and bent myself down. It was broad, narrowing to a point, a scaly, light brown something. I didn't want to believe it, but it was without doubt the tail of a lizard. I had read somewhere that a gecko can discard its tail and straightaway grow back a new one. The voracity of these tiny animals frightened me. I searched the walls for my pair of geckos but didn't find them. I fetched myself another Lal from the rattling fridge. I thought about the sun in the pores of the stones of Bellapais. I snapped the book shut. I did not yet know that after Mark had sold the Harrison House at the end of the following summer I would rent a house in Bellapais for my last Cypriot summer;

and I also could not yet guess that the geckos of Bellapais would be even more delicate and trusting than their fellows in Lapithos.

Famagusta and Salamis

Famagusta is a place of a thousand legacies. But it is also a place of forgetting, of obliteration, of death. From the remains of the palace of the Venetian governor we looked out over a Gothic ghost town, leached out, deeply tanned, rotten. Some houses in all the ruination were still inhabited, leaning up against the decay, patched up and repaired, with rusty satellite dishes on little balconies and flaking roofs. But these Turkish dwellings, inhabited in part by settlers from Anatolia, together with a meagre café, nestling in a Gothic archway, only deepened the impression of decline. It was difficult to conceive that this city had in the early Middle Ages been one of the richest and most important cities of the entire Levant and that its mighty, now crumbling, battlements and bastions had enclosed the luxurious palaces of trading dynasties and – or so the writers tell us – 365 churches, one for each day of the year.

The old chronicles bulge with stories from the period. They tell of a Count of Jaffa, who kept five hundred hunting dogs, and one servant for every two of these hounds, 'to bathe, comb and rub ointment into them'. Many of the aristocrats in Famagusta had at least two hundred servants, including falconers and huntsmen. The German priest Ludolf von Sudheim writes in his *Excerpta Cypria* of 1350 of a French knight who judged the bridal jewellery of one Famagusta noblewoman to far outstrip in value all the precious objects belonging to the Queen of France. In his chronicle, Leontios Machairas reports that the businessman Francis Lakhas not only gave his guests pearls as going-away presents but also had emeralds and rubies pulverised and then sprinkled onto the game at his evening banquets, like green and red salt. Which is to say nothing of the courtesans, of whom 'some possess more than 100,000 florins', and who built a chapel in honour of their patron saint to ease their consciences. The travel writers of the past may have been – in contrast to ourselves – braggarts, fantasists, to a greater or lesser extent. But even if we assume their stories are only half true, they give stunning testimony to Famagusta's golden age.

How did this wealth, this unspeakable luxury arise? The Crusaders, after losing many skirmishes, had lost their enthusiasm for the Holy Land. They concentrated their efforts on founding their own kingdoms in the neighbouring lands and islands. The French house of Lusignan had its eyes on Cyprus. The first of the dynasty, Guy de Lusignan, bore the title 'Seigneur de Chypre'. He had, it's true, also been crowned King of Jerusalem, but he had lost the Holy City to the Saracens after being defeated at the Battle of Hattin in 1187. His successor, Amaury de Lusignan, retained the right to the royal crown from the Holy Roman Emperor, Henry VI. This first Cypriot Lusignan exhausted his energies in futile attempts to retake the throne of Jerusalem. But as life became ever worse for the Crusaders in Syria and the few remaining territories in Palestine, so Cyprus grew more prosperous. Famagusta's real boom began with the Crusaders' devastating defeat at the Siege of Acre in 1291. The Lusignan King Henri II granted asylum to the fleeing businesspeople and bankers. Suddenly Famagusta was the only secure deep harbour left to Christendom in the Levant. From then on, trade poured through Famagusta. Little by little, the Kingdom of the Lusignans won for itself a voice in the concert of the European nations, out of all proportion to the size and population of the island.

Soon the island was of not merely economic and military significance. The Lusignans evolved from battle-hardened warriors into sophisticated despots, who wanted to catch up in every aspect of life with their French motherland and the city-states of Italy. Thus Bellapais Abbey and the cathedrals at Nicosia and Famagusta are quite the equals in daring and architectural skill of the cathedrals of Reims and Chartres. Men of letters like Philippe de Novare, Guillaume de Machaut and Philippe de Mézières wrote verses here and held a respectable rank in the pantheon of literature. Various European authors, such as Thomas Aquinas and Giovanni Boccaccio, dedicated works to the 'Kings of Cyprus'. It is said that by the beginning of the 14th century more than 70,000 people were living in Famagusta – Paris and Rome had not very many more inhabitants in the same period. Visitors who came from those great Western cities were stunned by the prosperity and opulence in Cyprus. Evidently, for the ruling class, excess was the norm. Perhaps an epigram from the time captures the atmosphere best: 'The insolent pride of France, the softness of Syria and the supple cunning of the Greeks – how clearly they emerge on this island!'

Just when the Lusignans had reached the zenith of their power and were teaming up with the Knights Templar and the Knights Hospitaller of Rhodes to launch high-spirited assaults on the coastal cities of Egypt and Anatolia, so their downfall began. It began – as if in a bad comedy – with a faux pas. It had become the custom of the Lusignans to have themselves crowned King of Cyprus in Nicosia and King of Jerusalem – a hollow anachronism! – in Famagusta. During the ceremony, envoys from Genoa and Venice would walk on either side of the king, holding onto the reins of his horse. At the coronation of Peter II in 1372, the representative of Venice suddenly grabbed hold of the rein on the right-hand side, which had always before been the prerogative of the Genoese. This argument over protocol escalated, leading to asinine and deadly brawls. Peter II took Venice's side, at which Genoa dispatched a fleet. The Genoese sacked the larger Cypriot cities and kept Famagusta under their control for nearly a hundred years. The city never recovered from this plundering and in 1473 fell into the hands of the Venetians, who took over the entire island. Their predominantly military rule was not broken until 1570 when a vast Turkish invading army, led by the infamous Lala Mustafa Pasha, attacked Nicosia, Kyrenia and the rest of the island. It was the definitive end of Latin supremacy. Only Famagusta resisted heroically for a further eleven months, until finally its Venetian captain, Marcantonio Bragadin, was forced to surrender.

The Venetian monk Calepio gives such a forceful account of the ferocity of the conquerors that I have to pass it on here. First of all, Lala Mustafa had all the soldiers and

Frankish citizens of Famagusta hacked to pieces before Bragadin's eyes. Then Bragadin himself was flayed alive right in front of the cathedral, which we had been looking at from the collapsed window arch of the Provveditore's palace. Even after his death, Calepio tells us, the Turks would not leave Bragadin's corpse in peace. The flayed skin was stuffed with straw, sat astride a cow and led through the city's streets, before eventually – as if that were not enough – being tied to the yardarm of a galley, which sailed back and forth in front of the harbour. Finally, it was 'dispatched to the Sultan in Constantinople, together with the severed heads of the other commanders.' Many years later, Bragadin's brothers and sons purchased back the skin for a high price and took it from Constantinople to Venice, where to this day, in an urn in the church of Santi Giovanni e Paolo, it has its rest.

After its conquest by the Turks the city fell into decline. The new occupiers used some buildings as prisons and laid waste to every church that they did not convert into a mosque. The Greek Orthodox population had to leave the city and settle to the south of its walls. This new city became known as Varosha – suburb – while the Greeks to this day generally use the oldest name for Famagusta itself, Ammóchostos – sunken into the sand. It was, however, in the middle of the 19th century that the old city suffered the worst damage, as the builders of Port Said needed materials for the construction of wharves and new hotels and so tore down entire churches and palaces and transported them back to Egypt. Varosha was to blossom only a century later. The wealthy Greeks – such as Niki Marangou's uncle

Mitsos – built large villas right on the bay; many hotels rose up, and tourism began in the grand style; a kind of cosmopolitan life filled this new Greek city. But after the Turkish invasion of 1974, this dream too melted away.

From the dilapidated houses and ruins of the medieval city we looked at the area sealed off by the Turkish army, no longer inhabited and decomposing in the salty wind and the sun. A city of phantoms.

'Do you think we can learn something from all these downfalls?' asked Karin. We were standing in front of the Cathedral of Saint Nicholas, where the Lusignans had been crowned and which now bore the name of the commander of Cyprus's Turkish conquerors, Lala Mustafa. A tiny minaret has been grafted onto the left of the cathedral's two towers, like some shy attempt at mastery over such a quantity of soaring Frankish Gothic.

I shook my head. The only thing to learn here in Famagusta was transience. But I didn't say that. I said that, to me, the most remarkable thing in life seemed to be that we almost never tap into our capacity for self-destruction. We may be tempted to, we may dream of it, but some ray of light, some turning of the wind, dissuades us. Why I said that, I do not know. We had delayed our trip to Famagusta until Karin arrived, because Famagusta had seemed to us like something promised, the guarantee of contact with past glory, the possibility of experiencing some great memory. Now we were striding across brown, uncultivated fields towards the harbour and the sea. The churches jutted out from among the Turkish houses; some were mere fragile shells, others had survived more or less intact. Their towers and turrets stretched up into the sky like unheard prayers. Two pomegranate trees shaded the remains of a chapel with an elegant portico of white marble. Perhaps this was the little church of the courtesans where they performed their strenuous penance. Or such was my fantasy. It was in the end the church of Saint George of the Greeks that snapped me out of my thoughts of destruction and self-destruction. The Orthodox Christians had built it as their Episcopal church, a counter-design to the Latin cathedral very close by. The church married together the Gothic and the Byzantine. Even half destroyed, its fallen-in dome overgrown with oleander and palm, its weighty splendour was still apparent. The still-surviving buttresses, which had once carried this Byzantine weightiness, gave an indication of the strength and breadth of the nave and made peace with the fallen city.

We arrived at the sea bastions. At the 'Gate of the Sea', which leads into the citadel, the winged white lion of Venice greeted us with his perky little tongue poking out from between his canine teeth. Another lion, carved in relief and beautifully weathered, with his paw on an opened book, waited for us at the entrance to the fortress known as 'Othello's tower'. Shakespeare's tragedy takes place in a 'Sea-Port in Cyprus', which probably means the real Famagusta – and the 'original' Othello is likely a former Venetian governor, Cristoforo Moro. Though 'Moro' actually means 'mulberry' rather than 'moor'; it's only Shakespeare's imagination that made him black for us.

'Why do the lions in Venice fly?' asked Anna.

'This lion looks like he's completely in a daze,' said Andrea.

'Perhaps the endless breakers did it?' speculated Karin. 'Anyway Cyprus's other lions are more charming. The lions of the Lusignans, prancing about on their crests and their gravestones, and the two lions of Richard the Lionheart have a heraldic dignity – even with that stylised grin.'

'But the lions from Venice have the great advantage of having wings,' I threw in.

The children performed gymnastics all the way along the ramparts, with their thin crenellations like tall hats. The round, inert citadel felt to me like a huge mausoleum. Through the slits left for the archers and their arrows we looked out at the sea, the waves and their unrelenting movement.

'And now – to Salamis!' shouted Karin. There were black deck chairs and sunshades printed on her white linen dress. On our short journey along the coast we stopped off at a kiosk by the side of the road and bought Coca-Cola, goat's cheese, olives and a flatbread. They didn't really have anything else.

You could say that Salamis was the forerunner of Ammóchostos and Famagusta. For a long time the queen among the ancient city-states, she had shown the best way to deal with both the booms and the disasters, until in the 7th century first earthquakes and then Arab invaders razed her to the ground. Many of her columns, friezes, capitals and dressed stones are still to be found today in the villages in the surrounding area and in the old city of Famagusta.

We stopped in front of a wire-mesh fence above the yellow sandy beach. It was broken through in many places and no longer served any purpose. Our view was of a vast plain, overgrown with shrubs and trees. Sections of wall and rows of columns rose up from the foliage. Vassos Karageorghis had told me in Nicosia that the old city covered a vast area. Almost 90 per cent of the ancient city still lay under the earth, buried among debris, sand and roots. Only the largest of the Roman and Byzantine remains, such as the gymnasium and palaestra, had been exposed; the rest had been overgrown by mimosa trees, which the English had planted to put a stop to the ravenous sand dunes.

We drifted about. The cicadas were screeching. The ruins sat there. A wind came off the sea and the air crackled like blue cellophane. From the gymnasium we wandered along a colonnaded street up to the amphitheatre, as yet unexcavated, which would have seated 17,000 spectators. A few marble statues were still standing. Generous behinds, well-rounded arms. But where were their hands? Their heads? Had they rolled away into the sea? Been struck off by Muslim iconoclasts? Or had UN soldiers carried them off back to Gothenburg or Essex? We were excited by the numerous holes on either side of the ancient street, made by excavation teams who had presumably had to cease their work in 1974. In the blink of an eye we became wannabe-archaeologists, forgot about everything else around us and scrabbled in the soil with penknives or our bare fingernails. We struck it lucky too! Anna dug out iridescent pieces of glass from vases or tear jugs; Andrea found pieces of mosaic and a badly damaged copper coin, covered in verdigris.

My most beautiful discovery was a large, curved potsherd, clearly from a jug, painted in a deep red with a garland of three stylised hearts, which ended at the edge of the sherd. I gave it to Karin.

We became ever more obsessed with our digging, and would happily have never moved again. But Vassos had planted a seed in my head: that Salamis's best sight of all was the 6th-century Kampanopétra Basilica. Salamis had enjoyed a second heyday under Byzantine rule: an immense water supply system and numerous early Christian basilicas bore witness to the prosperity of the city, resurrected after multiple earthquakes, a city which had already had in the time of the Romans more than 100,000 inhabitants. Vassos had told me all this in Nicosia, but it was the Kampanopé-tra church he had commended to me far beyond everything else. It was for one thing, purely on the basis of its dimensions – 120 metres long by 35 metres wide – one of the most monumental early Byzantine sacred buildings in the entire Mediterranean world. For another, it had exceptionally unusual mosaic floors, of small, irregularly cut pieces of marble, co-ordinated by colour and formed into staggering geometrical patterns.

I left my family at their excavations and set off on my search. Vassos had told me that the Basilica was located three kilometres along the coast in the direction of Fama-gusta, near to the marble Forum. I dragged myself through bushes and thorny scrubland. Hundreds of tiny white snail shells encrusted the dry twigs. Grasshoppers took to the air, stretching out their violet wings and showing me the way. Finally I came to a grove of mimosas where the lower layers of earth were exposed and the walls indicated the out-lines of aisles and a semicircular apse. I saw the first mosaic floors as well, a different one for each space and of ever more complex form and structure. Then I found a mosaic in the form of a circle, situated somewhat below the floor level of the main church, a disintegrated labyrinth with rays in the form of wings, recurring, rediscovering each other, fitting together into a single huge wing, wings into one wing, rays into one ray.

I sat myself down on the grass next to the mosaic. Suddenly it was as if that manifold wing was speaking to me in a soft, unchanging voice. I wanted to get to know the body behind this circle of wings. I wanted to test the air on which this garland of wings hovered. Within minutes, this wing in its manifold movement had won for me an urgency, a quick-wittedness, which I lacked. I studied the repetition of the feathers, the rays, the wing-beats. Through this movement the terrain around me became one unique space under one sky, blue since the time of its creation. I saw the feathers in tight clusters, the long flight feathers and the light black of the wing tips. For a long time I could not free myself from it, until I saw the real birds in the trees, exulting and then soaring away.

Diplomatic circles

Ninety-two thousand, seven hundred and ninety-nine pounds, eleven shillings and three pence: that was the compensation the British paid to the Ottoman Empire each year for Cyprus. The Prime Minister in London, old Disraeli, having bought up the Suez Canal, could make good use of this 'key to the eastern Empire'. This figure went through my head as the representatives of the European embassies in Nicosia sat down with the British ambassador, and in rotation offered their advice on the progress of the Cyprus question. As ever, we observed that there was no progress. The Turkish side wanted a federal state with a weak central government. The Greek Cypriots thought this an outrageous demand. After all, they constituted 80 per cent of the population of the entire island, and since the invasion they held only 63 per cent of the territory. The United Nations conducted separate talks, sometimes with the Cypriot president Glafkos Klerides, sometimes with the representative of the Turkish Cypriot ethnic group, Rauf Denktaş. Nothing moved. A suggestion from the former Secretary-General of the United Nations, Javier Pérez de Cuéllar, that at least Varosha, that abandoned city of hotels, should be given back to the Greeks – as a 'confidence-building measure' – was rejected by the Turkish side. Such moves could only be part of a comprehensive agreement. For the Greek islanders, it was another bitter disappointment.

'I've been here for three years now, and I still don't understand the Cypriots at all. It's depressing. I look them in the eye, they look me in the eye. It's a pointless exercise,' muttered the Frenchman, whose previous posting had been in New York – he was now bored to death. He was a congenial hedonist. But permissiveness and debauchery belonged to Cyprus's ancient past, and today were only chimeras. Every day he waited for notification of his transfer.

'The terrible thing is, I don't believe in a political solution any more,' interjected our British colleague and host. 'If one is possible at all, it can only be with these people, through these people. And yet they're almost militantly indifferent to each other. The Greek Cypriots simply deny what the Turkish Cypriots are feeling, what they believe in, hope for, are afraid of. And vice versa. The indifference is the real evil. Not the positions in Ankara and Athens.'

'What would the situation be today if the Turkish invasion had never happened? Endless guerrilla war from Grivas and his EOKA, assassinations and attacks? Or would the entire island have been incorporated into Greece?' asked our Spaniard, who kept an eye on his official duties from Beirut and was here for work.

The Italian representative in our circle, a lively, always elegantly dressed Neapolitan, took refuge in an anecdote. In the most critical days of July 1974, after the junta in Athens had installed Nikos Sampson as President in Nicosia, one Western ambassador – or so the story went – had initiated the evacuation of all his country's tourists and put the possessions of those of his citizens who lived on the north coast facing Turkey in safe storage at the ambassador's residence.

Bülent Ecevit had flown to London. For three long days, nothing happened. The ambassador spent his days on the embassy roof with a pair of binoculars, scanning the sky over the Kyrenia Mountains. Back home, people were already criticising his behaviour. Were these specially arranged flights really necessary? Wasn't evacuation too expensive and completely premature? On the morning of the third day the ambassador saw hundreds of opened parachutes floating in the blue sky over Kyrenia and strode, relieved, to the ticker machine to send the message that 'On the 20 July 1974, the military invasion backed by Turkey has just begun, north of Kyrenia.' Later he would describe what he had seen from the roof of his embassy, saying that it was as if an invisible hand had been sprinkling pepper onto the Kyrenia Mountains.

Those days of high tension, the two waves of violent land grabs, the Turkish troops pushing right into the heart of Nicosia, were ten years later almost impossible to imagine, so successfully had the Greek Cypriots made the best of their painful situation. As I walked back from the British Embassy to our house on Gladstonos Street, past supermarkets, past office blocks clad in mirrored glass, past large blocks of flats, avoiding the old city with its sandbags, walls and barbed wire, the city, or the southern part of it at least, seemed prosperous and ordered to the point of tedium. The summer was over, the pavements were lively, the cafés overflowing. The cinema hoardings were flashing. We had left Lapithos a few days before, and had handed the house keys back to Mark. The prospect of spending next summer back in the Harrison House had not made our farewells any easier.

I was sitting on the terrace of the villa I had rented in Nicosia. The villa stood in one of the first residential areas to be established outside the city walls, around the end of the 19th century, at the same time as the Archaeological Museum, the Public Theatre and the City Park, which were all nearby. To this day Gladstonos Street contains a number of beautiful, grand houses in the English colonial style, with tall white columns flanking the entranceway, houses that you might find in the best quarters of Athens, Alexandria, Genoa or London. Our house was not one of these. It had been built in the 1940s, in late Bauhaus style, chunky and angular. Its sole virtues were that it had been built entirely of the honey-yellow local sandstone and that it was half-obscured by old palm trees and hibiscus bushes.

I was waiting for my friend George Lanitis. He was my historian for all things Nicosian. There are cities – we all know them – which bewitch us from the beginning, from our first approach, our first entrance. Nicosia is not among them. Though by now I knew several squares, residential streets and buildings that I liked very much, nothing had made an intimate connection with me. Eighty years ago, Nicosia must still have been a beautiful city. Its defensive walls, laid out in a star, had enclosed a settlement built entirely of yellow-brown sandstone, a city of Ottoman gracefulness, whose teeming roofscape mixed domes and minarets with palm trees and the twin towers of the Agia Sophia Cathedral. Back then it must still have been possible to make out the much older fortified city of the Lusignan dynasty. I imagined life in that medieval Nicosia to be just as cheerful and luxurious as that in Famagusta.

As I pictured them, the knights were joyful and carefree figures, always in the mood for hunting, with birds in their hair, men who, after they pulled off their chain mail vests, plunged never their swords but only their members into the perfumed laps of courtesans.

'Long, long ago!' commented George, in English, on my fantasies. He was in a good mood that evening. In order to forget about his house in Bellapais, which had been occupied by a senior Turkish officer, he had built a new house 40 miles from Nicosia, near to a wine-growing village, more or less mimicking the volumes of the old house. He had just returned from his new property and was gleefully rubbing together his large, brown, thickly haired hands.

'We planted two palms today, in front of the house, one male and one female. Both of them are twenty years old. Cost me a fortune, buying them and getting them brought over from Limassol. But they already look like they've been there forever. And they'll fertilise each other and we'll have a load of little palm trees!' He grinned into his wine glass. 'And I'm going to buy the vineyard right next to our land. I've already had the labels designed. That was a lot of fun! Nuits Saint-Georges and Château Kalo-Chorio. You know the village is called Kalo-Chorio?'

I nodded. 'I will visit your château soon,' I said.

George was so filled with his plans that it was a delight to watch him. He stroked his walrus moustache, brushed his eyebrows with his left index finger, made grand hand gestures and pushed great wafts of the evening's jasmine in my direction. In his zeal he had completely forgotten that his entire building project had such an unhappy cause.

'And did I tell you,' he whispered conspiratorially, 'that I'm extending the cellar into a vast loft-style space. I'll be able to show my photos there. Nowadays artists don't just need a gallery, they have to have their own showroom, not just so they can show their art' – he paused significantly – 'but so they can make direct contact with their buyers. With you.'

It was a joke with undertones. I had still not bought a photograph off George. Now he turned to me and said: 'Are you a temporary bachelor again? Where's Karin? What are you up to? What can I do to get you to finally fall in love with Nicosia?' George knew that I had difficulties with the Cypriot capital. I had been to Cyprus once before as a tourist, in the spring of 1974, before the Turkish occupation. Back then an atmosphere of past cosmopolitanism still pervaded the old city, however weakly. Since the savagery of partition, that atmosphere didn't work any more. Since then the city had been living in two halves, the business-oriented, efficient Greek portion and the oriental, lethargic Turkish, where the life was mostly to be found in the inner courtyards of houses or on the main roads out towards Kyrenia.

'I do forget the division sometimes, like you do,' I said to George, 'but then it's there again, a visible scar, a divine warning. Maybe it's because it's surrounded by the bland, flat, empty, non-descript Mesaoria plain, but the city seems to me to be haunted by its trauma. Or at the least, there's never a good atmosphere.'

'But that's totally untrue!' objected George. 'It's not true any more, at any rate. Just look at all the young people, the artists, the architects, the designers. They've breathed new life into those Venetian walls. Famagusta Gate is a centre for theatre, performance, dance, music. Think of Arianna and her choreography. Think of the exhibitions by Stass, Kouroushis. They're amazing!' He jumped up from his chair and puffed himself out. 'There are even a few imaginative guys who've been equipping the dead zone right next to the Green Line with bars. All the high life is getting in the way of the military. That's a real kick, when the UN jeeps on their patrols struggle to get past all the tables full of bottles. You know, for me, something damn near a utopia is emerging: that's what it could be, once the partition is lifted and all the damage is put right.'

I fetched another bottle of wine and the remains of an orange cake from the fridge.

'This is a stunner,' I said to George and pushed a piece of the cake towards him. 'Chrystalla made it, our cleaner. She cooks the oranges and then purées them with the peel, mixes in beaten egg whites, sugar and ground almonds. Then you put the mix into the oven for one hour. It tastes delicious and it goes well with wine.'

'Hmm, you're right.' George was chewing appreciatively. 'It's sweet and sour and bitter!'

'Like Nicosia?'

'Well, my friend, this city is like a cake with many layers. You mustn't look at our city as a city. Probably not as a cake either. And probably not as a stranded ship, with a hundred cargoes in its belly. Best to think of it as a space for the most diverse of conversations. And if you're sick of the city, you always have the rest of the island, which is completely peppered with monasteries and churches and ruins. In every monastery they'll tell you a dozen strange legends about their patron saint. For me, more than anything, Cyprus consists of legends, stories and customs. It's almost unbelievable how it's all survived from the ancient past. The line from Aphrodite to Mary is short and uninterrupted.'

'There are continuities and interruptions. Last week we were witnesses to a circumcision celebration, in the middle of Lapithos village square. This little boy was lying on a vast bed under the wide open sky, pretty terrified ...'

'That's a tough ordeal for the Turkish boys. But for us, for the Orthodox, baptism is a test to destruction. Every Greek man carries the mark of it around with him. A deep imprint on the subconscious. Here in Nicosia the ritual has died out a bit, but in the countryside! I promise you: out there, there's a copper vat of hot water sitting in the middle of the church, a priest with a bushy black beard, candles, soap, scissors and gruesome relatives from every corner of the earth – the uncle from Lagos who's a car dealer, another one from Athens, he's a plumber, and so on. And it starts long before the actual baptism, with a series of, what should I call them, prophylactic rituals. The baby has to be covered in salt, so that he'll grow up strong and can't later be accused of 'not having been properly salted'. His nails mustn't be cut for six months, otherwise he'll become a thief. Then the nails are cut at the baptism and the father must keep the clippings in his wallet for forty days, so that the child being baptised will have plenty of money once he's grown up. The child has to drink his very first sip of water from the shell of a swallow's egg. Then he'll be eloquent. And there should be seven almonds put into his first bath, which later he has to eat, or bury in the ground. And at the baptism itself the godfather has to spit on the ground, to disassociate the child from the devil.'

'And did your godfather spit on the ground, George, when you were baptised?'

'Who knows! I don't remember anything about it. I only know that I howled mightily in all directions, without a break, from long before the brutal priest undressed me and scalded me in the water. That's what I've been told. And that the priest made the sign of the cross on my red, spotty face with an oil which had been sent especially by the Patriarch in Constantinople.'

'Voodoo!'

'And' – continued George – 'he cut off three locks of my hair with a pair of scissors and gave them to my grandmother. In this way a new Greek Christ will be brought into the world.'

'You describe it beautifully. I can smell the wax, the oil, the incense, your mother's perfume. I imagine her perfume smelled of softened almond biscuits?'

'That was nearly fifty years ago. Hard to grasp. Cyprus has changed so completely, with the mass tourism here in the South and Turkish imperialism in the North. But these ceremonies, if you go into the villages of the Troodos, they still survive. Sometimes I think that surrealism was invented here on Cyprus. Have you heard about Saint Spyridon? The patron saint of basket-weavers? He's often depicted with a basket on his head. He was a shepherd boy and then, in the blink of an eye, a bishop. He was so eloquent that all the other prelates hated him. At the Council of Nicaea he impressed all the delegates by giving a completely concrete explication of the nature of the Holy Ghost. One day, his rivals cut the heads off his two donkeys – he had a black donkey and a white one – while he was asleep. When he woke up he put the heads back on the donkeys, absolutely no problem, but his mind was somewhere else, already on his next sermon, because he put the head of the white donkey on the neck of the black donkey and the head of the black one onto the white. And so these two strange, checkered donkeys carried him to the next monastery. By the way, Niki is a treasure trove. She knows so much about the old legends, all these old rituals. A hundred stories for every saint. You should stick close to her.'

'I like Niki a lot,' I said. 'And you know why? She radiates, I think, a sanguine melancholy.'

A cat with dove-grey fur darted across the terrace. Its darting seemed to raise a benevolent night wind. The old palms creaked softly.

'We aren't particularly melancholy here,' remarked George. 'In the Levant, the dominant qualities are a mix of cunning, impatience and exaggeration. We agree with the old Danish philosopher: "Life is lived forward, and understood backwards." Kierkegaard. He meant us, without having met us.'

I shared out the rest of the wine fraternally into our two glasses. We emptied them in a single gulp.

A small bag of salt and a
terracotta phallus

Ever since I saw the black cult stone of Kouklia, I could not get it out of my mind. I visited it again and again, in Room VIII of the Museum of Cyprus. For two reasons: most obviously, this large, unprepossessing, dully gleaming stone – some believe it to be a meteorite – held some kind of allure for me, which it lacked for the other museum visitors, who walked past without noticing it. And then there was the fact that the museum was just a short walk from our house on Gladstonos Street. The Garden Café opposite the museum was part of the appeal too. It was a lovely place, just on the other side of the street, wreathed in jasmine and oleander trees, where I was fond of retreating to read, when the embassy had closed and the children were still in their English pre-school. If I was weary of reading, I walked over the street and visited the stone. It is roughly conical in shape. We are told that it comes from Kouklia, the ancient sanctuary of Aphrodite near Paphos. We are told that for centuries the goddess was worshipped in the form of this stone. It is worth reading J.G. Frazer's classic *The Golden Bough* on the subject of these conical stones in the Middle East. Frazer explains that, before the Phoenicians arrived at what is now Kouklia, the first settlers venerated 'their' fertility goddess, Baalaath or Astarte, in the form of a conical stone or a pyramid. These conical cult stones, which were worshipped like idols, have also been found in Syria, Pamphylia and Malta. During the ceremonies the stone would be drenched and rubbed with olive oil, which is the source of its greenish shimmer, the dull gleam which has lasted to the present day.

Pilgrims had to pay a sum of money to gain entry to the sacred precinct. In return they received a small bag of salt, which symbolised Aphrodite's emergence from the waves, and a terracotta phallus. When they were not praying, the pilgrims spent their time with the women who – as the rituals demanded – had to surrender themselves to a stranger before they could marry. The payment for this love service went to the goddess. The whole set-up must have lent a nun-like odour to these temporary prostitutes. One of Vassos's colleagues, who often saw me skulking around the cult stone, told me that Kouklia, the Mycenaean colony of ancient Paphos, had been the centre of a thriving 'pilgrimage industry' – that was his expression – for almost a thousand years, thanks to Aphrodite and her lover Adonis. Sensing my interest in the Aphrodite cult, he led me into his office. He offered me tea and a battered armchair beneath a huge, badly faded photo of the gymnasium at Salamis.

'The story of Kinyras,' he commenced, 'is more interesting than Aphrodite, who, let's face it, we don't know much about anyway.'

'Kinyras?'

'Kinyras was one of the first kings of Paphos. Tied up with Aphrodite. He proclaimed himself high priest and founded her cult. A highly profitable business. This Kinyras married the daughter of Pygmalion, the one who fell in love with a statue and took it to bed with him. Kinyras is said to have had three daughters by her, and then copulated with Adonis in the form of one of his own daughters. Thus he established a pattern of worship and incest, which was to distinguish the entire dynasty of high priests for hundreds of years.'

'Incest?' I interrupted him. 'Was that a threesome? Or some kind of homosexuality?'

'In my opinion, a threesome,' said the museum curator, who now introduced himself as Konstantis. 'In those days, everything was permitted.' And then he picked up his thread again: 'So, this Kinyras also played a part in Greek politics, during the Trojan wars. For example, he sent a breastplate to Agamemnon, covered in snakes of worked silver. Later on he sent him fifty ships, though admittedly forty-nine of them were models made of clay. He was so rash that he decided to take on Apollo in a contest. He lost. The poor man had to pay for that with his life.'

Rarely had I heard so many mad stories in such rapid succession.

'How much of that is true? Half of it?' I asked.

'It's all documented. Inscriptions, papyruses, mosaics.' He rummaged around in his desk and dragged out a book. 'Here,' he said, and rapped on the wine-red binding. 'By an Italian archaeologist. He spent years researching the Kinyras dynasty. The sons and the sons of sons and all their descendants were divine prince consorts to Aphrodite. They slept with the temple whores. They led lives of luxury, surrounded by flatterers in their service.'

'And what happened next?'

'The arrival of the Ptolemies signalled the end of the dynasty. Indeed, the end of all the small Greek kingdoms on Cyprus. But Paphos continued to be the religious centre of the island. The Romans didn't change that at all. It was Christianity that finally brought about the downfall of the Aphrodite cult. You know, presumably, that it was Saint Barnabas from Salamis and the Apostle Paul, who had travelled to Paphos, who converted the Roman Governor Sergius Paulus. Cyprus was the first country to be ruled by a Christian. What happened in Cyprus back then was the best propaganda for the new faith!'

Konstantis lit up a cigarette and looked through the smoke at the ceiling fan, which was rotating languidly.

'The crazy thing is,' he continued, 'the transition from heathen cult to Christianity was pretty much painless. In fact, it happened almost without anyone noticing. The inhabitants of Kouklia have carried on pouring olive oil onto the stones of the Temple of Aphrodite once a year, up into our own time, just as the early pilgrims anointed the conical stone with oil. Only now it's in the name of the Virgin Mary. There's a lovely story about a priest from Pissouri, who reassured someone travelling to Paphos: "They don't call her Aphroditissa any more, they call her Chrysopolitissa now."'

He stubbed out his cigarette, stowed the book away in a drawer and pulled out a little bottle of ouzo.

'To finish?' he said.

I'd never drunk this aniseed spirit undiluted before. Firewater.

'You know,' said Konstantis, 'Aphrodite visits me

sometimes. Not in the winter, but in the spring, every week.' He looked at me. 'It's true!' he added emphatically.

After this conversation, at supper back home, I asked our little circle whether we shouldn't spend Christmas and New Year in Paphos, with excursions to Polis and the Akamas peninsula. On Karin's face I read approval. Anna and Andrea, by contrast, had just discovered the delights of lingering. Let's stay at home. Invite some little friends over. Swing on the swing behind the house, suspended between two orange trees.

I began circuitously: 'Paphos is famous the world over for three things. First of all, the cult of Aphrodite. That doesn't mean much to you, but Aphrodite – look, there's a picture of her on the wine label – was the great goddess of love. And she was said to be very, very beautiful. And somehow she's still alive now. Second, the Apostle Paul, you know him, he was one of Jesus's disciples, was tied to a column in Paphos and flogged, before he succeeded in converting the Roman Governor to Christianity. The column is still standing and we can inspect it. And thirdly, Paphos is famous for its pelican. He toddles around in the old harbour. There are actually postcards of him. He has tousled feathers on his head and beady orange eyes. And he's overweight, because the tourists are constantly feeding him, even giving him walnuts and marshmallows. His big throat pouch simply just takes it all in.'

'If that's how it is,' said Anna, 'then, OK. We'll come with you.'

Konstantis's tangled stories wouldn't leave me in peace.

I fetched the slightly tattered copy of Herodotus off the bookshelf. I knew that he too had been on Cyprus and had visited the area of Old Paphos. Apparently so many varying legends were entwined around Pygmalion, Kinyras and Adonis that not even Herodotus could disentangle them. But the sacred prostitution survived as part of the ritual into his time, that is, right into the classical period. 'Many wealthy women,' I read in Herodotus, 'who are too proud to mingle with the rest, travel to the temple in covered carriages, and then wait there with an entire host of servants ... Tall, beautiful women quickly manage to return home. But the ugly have to stay a long time before they can fulfill the law; some, indeed, for three or four years.'

Like a kiosk in the sea

The day after Christmas we drove via Pera Chorio and the monastery at Stavrovouni, which is visible for miles around, enthroned on a peak 700 metres high, to the main road from Larnaka to Limassol. I drove around Limassol. I had been there many times in an official capacity, visiting the representatives of German shipping companies, and every time I had found the city uninteresting, repulsive even, ugly. After the loss of Varosha, the Greek Cypriots had concentrated all their resources on Agía Nápa and especially on Limassol, steering business and tourism into this formerly sleepy harbour town with furious determination. The endless seafront street had been entirely blighted by vast chain hotels, cheap restaurants, casinos, amusement arcades and hastily erected apartment blocks. In these heaps of concrete, I had thought to myself on my first visit, you could see all the clearer what the island had forfeited in such a short time: harmony, sweetness, lustre. And what she had won: the sovereignty of beauty abolished and replaced with a new, cheap prosperity, which had no regard for light or landscape. Only much later, when I accompanied Niki for a reading she was giving to the Writers' Association there, did she show me the small, still surviving core of the old city. Here were a few beautiful buildings from the late 19th and early 20th centuries. A clique of Italian architects, almost all from Genoa or Milan, had erected these classical residential buildings across the entire Eastern Mediterranean at the turn of the last century. You can still find them today in Beirut, Jaffa, Alexandria, Tripoli and in Limassol. But these properties, grouped around a handful of streets and squares full of plane trees, seemed to have nothing to do with Limassol. They formed a tiny, unobserved oasis, encircled by abominations and threatened by the bulldozers of property speculators, poised to flatten them in an instant.

The castle of the Templars and the Knights of St John in Kolossi and the ruins of Kourion on its spit of land rising more than a hundred metres above sea level we were saving for our return journey. We were impatient to get to Paphos. In comparison to the north coast, with the dramatic Kyrenia Mountains, the coastline here was rather boring. Bluffs of white chalk alternated with green plains, mostly alluvial land from now-dried-up rivers, which had once run down from the Troodos massif. These plains were planted with vines, some vegetables and, here and there, where the green land blended into rocky hills, olive trees.

We did make a stop, however, at Aphrodite's Rock, a couple of miles before Kouklia. These two rocks, immortalised a million times over on postcards, are great lumps of limestone escarpment that have fallen into the sea. From the parking area set high up above them, they didn't seem like anything special. The children opted to stay in the car, so I climbed down the slope with Karin onto the stony shore and to the water's edge. The sun stood in the middle of the sky. The sea was calm, received the light, glittered. The love of the light for the sea made us alert. Alert to the lightning flashes from the waves, alert to the jibes of the rock doves, alert to the curve of the ever-darkening horizon. So it was here, as the legend goes, as the ancients never tired of telling, that Aphrodite rose up out of the foam. Hard to believe, but perhaps all that matters is that back then everyone believed it and that this bay here, now, for all time, is cloaked in this belief. Was it a priest of some earlier people who first formulated this myth, this birth of the goddess from the foam of the sea? Or was it a poet? In the Homeric Hymns it runs:

Of stately Aphrodite, gold-wreathed, beautiful,
I sing: mistress over every citadel on sea-girt Cyprus.
There the damp breath of the west wind brought her
over the waves of the loud moaning sea
on soft foam

I have always read these verses in a state of tremendous, unforgettable overwhelming. They make me believe what my rational mind cannot accept. Not far from this little bay with its two rocks her shrine was established, with its multitude of beautiful and tenacious and endless legends, as endless as this ungraspable, seaweed-rich water.

Of the immemorial temple city, the holy shrine, and the altars once bathed in incense and flowers, there was nothing left to see in Kouklia. The ruined city lacked even a fragment of magic, and the principal temple was shattered down to its foundations. The few remaining walls were head-high, nothing more. Carob trees spread their scrawny black branches out over the remains. It was hard work to form a picture. Even the archaeologists had found few substantial clues to a clear story. Almost all the pieces retrieved in the excavations at Kouklia were incomplete – stutters, syllables, half-sentences, hard to reassemble. Even the graves in the surrounding valleys had been plundered by robbers long before the archaeologists arrived. The sacred precinct had been devastated by a series of earthquakes during the reign of Emperor Theodosius, and the great temple complex had not been rebuilt since. Old Paphos had shrivelled into the village Kouklia, whose modest buildings seemed to me to be entirely patched together from the stones, ashlars and friezes of Aphrodite's Temple.

Nea Paphos, the new Paphos, was about ten kilometres away, in a westerly direction. The road snaked past a rocky spit of land, through fields of vegetables, ancient terraces and gnarly vines on trellises, as it likely had done in Roman and Crusader times. We checked in at a hotel on a hill above the harbour, not far from the sea. This hotel, built at the beginning of the 1970s, had at that time been the first large modern hotel in Paphos and, kitted out with all the conveniences, it should have remained so for some time. Since then, scarcely fifteen years later, this strip of coast too had been concreted over, unimaginative chain hotels rising up in both directions. But it was not as bad as Limassol.

We had dawdled away quite a long time in Kouklia, so it was already evening. We went looking for Poseidon, a simple restaurant, which George Lanitis had recommended to us and which lay a little higher up, in Ktima. Eventually we found it. The plump cook, Menelaus, didn't do anything fancy. Whatever he brought to the table was delicious: stuffed aubergines, hummus, yoghurt, warm flat bread from their own baker's oven in the backyard, and the freshest, most glorious swordfish I have ever eaten. It was dark by the time we got back to the hotel. I stepped out from our room onto the balcony, which looked out over the sea. To the left, across the flat roofs of the bungalows of the hotel nearest to us, the little harbour of Paphos glinted. The fort, built by the Turks in 1589, sat like a black cube on the shoulder of the harbour mole. A couple of fishing boats were setting out into the open sea with their navigation lights on. The overall effect was so calm, so sleepy that I had to work hard to imagine how countless pilgrims – some historians estimate that a million people came over the course of a millennium – had once landed here to visit the temple and worship the goddess, 'the great shame and glory of Cyprus' as the inimitable Rupert Gunnis, that uptight Brit, wrote. 'Glory for its buildings and treasure,' he asserted, 'shame from the unrestrained licenses of the priestesses, who wantonly flaunted their prostitution.'

After two days we had seen everything there was to see in Paphos: the pelican; the column to which Paul was allegedly shackled; the simple Byzantine church of Chrysopolitissa, successor to Aphrodite; and the underground church of Saint Solomoni. It was, paradoxically, only the lonely necropolis, stretched out along the seafront to the west for more than a kilometre, that gave us some sense that Paphos had been the capital city of the island around the end of the 4th century, in the time of the Ptolemies, the

Greek rulers of Egypt, and that the elite and sophisticated spirit of Alexandria had wafted here, in the statuary, the theatre, the festive processions. Many of these underground graves, hewn into the rock, had been destroyed by wind, sand and salt or ripped into the sea by the surf. But some were well-preserved, graves of royal proportions, veritable houses for the dead. We clambered down the steps into inner courtyards with foyers, whose columns and entablature supported the overgrown, rocky ground that lay above us. Here, deep under the earth, in the ornate surrounds of doors that no longer existed, in the elaborately worked friezes and the decorated tympana, a last remnant of the sometime luxury of the Ptolemies still glimmered. The corridors and shafts ramified into an uncanny subterranean city of the dead, stinking of bat droppings. Over our heads we heard the sea, a distant whispering.

'Travel well' – that was the commonest formula on the memorial stones for the dead.

We wanted to go on to Polis and the Akamas peninsula. But before our departure we asked the girls whether they had one more request. We feared we would have to pay a final visit to the mangy old pelican in the harbour or purchase a gigantic portion of pistachio ice cream from the cross-eyed ice-cream seller in the café opposite the hotel. No, they wanted to go one more time to the church of Saint Solomoni.

This church was the strangest of Paphos's monuments. A large Roman grave wrought out of massive stones, it had at some point been 'converted' and transformed into a tiny church. There were still remnants of old, painted frescoes and a stone iconostasis. But it wasn't the church itself that earnt the interest of Anna and Andrea. Next to the church stood a 'sacred spring'. The sick and the burdened, especially those suffering from diseases of the eye, came there, washed their clothes in the spring, tore off scraps of cloth and tied them onto the branches of a tree, which stood next to the steps down to the spring. This tree looked extraordinary – covered over and over with many-coloured scraps, it was a totem tree, a carnival tree, a huge talisman with a thousand tiny, fluttering flags. It was this tree that the children wanted to see one more time. They tied small red cloths, which they had purchased at the harbour, onto a bough. It was already so 'full' that they had to laboriously push some of the other knotted cloths together first.

After we had crested the mountain behind Paphos and swung down through the balmy bay of Chrysochoús, we took a rest stop at Polis. Tourism, taking hold here too, had bloated what once must have been a sleepy and half abandoned village into a small town. But now, in winter, all the bustle was gone. No one was looking for diving fins, or a surfboard, or sunglasses. Most of the shops along the tortuous road through the town were closed. On the hunt for a *kafeneion* we got lost in the side streets and here the old, rural Cyprus was still entirely present. In the nooks and crannies of backyards, nervous hens pecked, fluttering laundry dried in the weak sun and a cat played the role of gaping predator. Geraniums bloomed in rusted metal canisters and a jasmine bush strewed its intense scent in a blind rage.

We drove on towards Latsi. Latsi was not a village, not

even a hamlet. It was a tiny black dot on the map, exactly on the dividing line between light-blue and light-brown, in the middle of the curvature of the Chrysochoús bay. When you approached it, this dot consisted of a large empty barn on a kink in the road, three old warehouses for carob, a jetty with a landing stage on cement pilasters and – in front of the jetty – one small building and one larger one, which belonged to Yiangos and Peter. Both were fishermen and they operated a fish restaurant on the ground floor of the building next door. On the other side of the road, halfway into the scrub and built on a chalky hill, the first hotel in Latsi, called Elia Apartments, had just opened. We checked in. The evenings were cold and damp and yet we were lucky with the weather. In the middle of the day the sun shone so warmly that we could eat outside, directly above the landing stage. On the masts of the white-, blue- and red-painted fishing boats, flags of black plastic crackled in the wind. Yiangos explained that in a storm, when a ship gets into distress, these black flags are the easiest to make out.

'They flash black,' was how he expressed it.

The two sold what they took from the water in Polis. But we were allowed to inspect the fish and prawns and calamari first and pick out for ourselves the most beautiful bream and the most slippery squid. Peter was the cook. He didn't do much. He used simple ingredients – oil, fennel, lemon, garlic, salt – and threw the animals on the grill, or if they were small, like the red mullet, into a pan. It all tasted exquisite. The tiny prawns in a strong garlic sauce were, in Anna's opinion, 'super-delicious'.

We feasted, looking out over the large blue circle of the

water. Latsi radiated a happy abandonment. We felt so at ease that we stayed for a week and wandered around the as yet entirely unspoilt Akamas peninsula. The Cypriot parliament had designated it a nature reserve.

'Akamas is actually really under threat,' fulminated Peter at one jolly evening gathering. 'There's no respect for nature. Our revered foreign minister wants to personally circumvent the laws and erect a luxury hotel next to the Baths of Aphrodite.'

'We have to organise something,' interjected Yiangos. 'Leaflets. A demonstration. Even the people in Polis are against it. Against the corruption. Against this ferocious, senseless building, which has already spoilt Paphos.'

I suggested, without exactly believing it, that the addiction to profit, the drive for business, the rampant building could perhaps be explained as the Greek Cypriots seeking to forget the trauma of partition.

Lionel Miskin, an old Englishman, who, with his snow-white crown of hair, looked like Bertrand Russell, made superbly playful ceramics and had come from Paphos to visit us, said in his bone-dry way that there might be something in that.

'Cyprus is a little republic of madness,' he offered, chuckling.

We drank to that.

'To me, Cyprus seems like a kiosk in the sea, where you can buy everything.'

We drank to that too.

We were drinking the popular local white by the name of 'Aphrodite'. The yellow label showed the statue of Venus found at Soli, a pale brown torso above the name of the goddess in antique-style script. All the white wines in Cyprus had the names of goddesses.

'If I'm not drinking Aphrodite, I'm drinking Persephone,' I slurred to myself, making no connection to our previous topic.

But now Peter and Yiangos's pride had been touched.

'Cypriot wines are very good,' the two said in unison. 'And the wines from the slopes of the Troodos are the best in the world. No question! We request you, tomorrow morning, to drink a bottle of Persephone, while paying attention! This is serious for us!'

As we said goodbye the two men gave Anna and Andrea the sword from a large swordfish. They had sawn it off. It actually looked like a saw. It stank horribly, but the girls were proud of it and wouldn't be parted from it. We drove off, making one last detour to the 'Baths of Aphrodite', where the narrow road came to a stop, and we had one more *metrio* at the restaurant of the same name. I had forgotten how, already by mid-morning, the light here can gleam, even in winter. The water beneath us was turquoise. The dried-out ranks of mighty agave flowers were echoed in the black bushy stones at the bottom of the clear water. The colours changed as the sun rose higher. On the other side of the bay the Troodos mountains were a diaphanous rosy grey. This grey dwindled from minute to minute, as the fog rising off the sea grew thicker, until soon the shape of the mountains was only an afterimage on our retinas.

Centre and periphery

I couldn't believe my eyes. The first course was artichokes with a vinaigrette. All our guests were obediently biting off the fleshy lower part of the leaves and laying the rest on a large dish in the middle of the table, where a graceful pyramid was growing upwards. Except Glyn Hughes, who was consuming the leaves root and branch, so to speak, shoving them whole into his mouth and chewing them at great length, as his bushy black eyebrows jerked up and down. Was it possible that he – who was by then nearly 60 years old – had never before in his long life been confronted with an artichoke? We silently agreed to ignore it. We covered up for him.

After the seclusion of Latsi, we were in the mood for society. Straight after New Year we had invited a few friends to Gladstonos Street. Arianna Economou and Horst Weierstall came, Niki and her sister Anna Marangou, who was in charge of culture for the city council in Nicosia and worked closely with Lellos Demetriades, our neighbours Rita and Ioannis Sofocleus – and Glyn Hughes. A Welshman, Glyn had come to Cyprus at barely 25 years old, with a contract in his pocket to teach art at the junior school. He was, however, primarily a painter, as well as an art critic and especially a generator of ideas in the then still very sleepy Nicosia art scene. Together with the painter Savva, who had studied in Paris with André Lhote, he had established the first ever art gallery on the island. He himself was a fierce colourist. Distorted figures – he adored Francis Bacon – and jagged landscapes were the dominant motifs of his painting in the years we knew each other. He was undoubtedly a great talent. Alongside everything else, he also designed vast stage sets for the local state theatre and generally busied himself everywhere. Now he was sitting at our table, in a purple and green batik shirt which he had made himself, consuming his artichoke not *comme il faut*. Rita Sofocleus, who I didn't especially like, attempted to distract attention from the situation by telling a joke in her deep, throaty voice.

'So,' she commenced, 'a man goes to his doctor. The doctor says that things are looking very bad for him. He has only three months left to live. What should I do, moans the man. Don't drink, don't go to any parties, don't have sex and don't smoke, says the doctor. What good will that do? asks the sick man. The doctor replies: the three months will seem very, very long.'

Her husband laughed the loudest. He had been in the oil industry for a long time, worked for BP in Kuwait and Iran, had seen everything, experienced everything. Now, in his retirement, he simply wanted to have a good time. Every morning I would see him on his balcony near to our house, lovingly cleaning his shotgun, peering down each of the two barrels in turn. Nevertheless, I liked him. He was a drinker, he was sharp-tongued and he always kept his cool. Now he was laughing.

'How often have you heard that joke, Ioannis?' asked

Niki, a little irritated. We had determined at the beginning of the evening that this one time we would avoid the cursed politics; but plainly that didn't mean pathetic jokes were on the agenda.

'There's an insight in every joke,' was my attempt at mediation.

For Arianna this seemed like a good moment to tell us about her latest project, a dance piece with video, working title: *The Silence of Eurydice*. She wanted to perform it at various locations in the 'buffer zone' and dedicate it to the missing people on the island.

'Oh no! Not politics again!'

'Whatever we do here is politics!'

Horst disagreed. In his paintings and drawings he pursued the secrets of nature, of the animal. I had just bought a large oil painting from him. A fabulous beast took up almost the entire canvas, half Pegasus, half enormous and yet delicate butterfly. To me the picture seemed a happy hybrid of Joseph Beuys and Odilon Redon, and yet entirely original.

'The problem is that the island is too small,' said Horst. 'There are no collectors, no museums, no art critics.'

'What?' said Glyn.

'You're a great critic, Glyn, but who reads the arts pages of the *Cyprus News*, which at best consist of a half page every third day? And what kind of distribution do you have?'

'This attitude does us no good,' Anna interjected. 'We just end up ogling Athens. As if Athens was the gateway to the world! The Cypriot artist's late desire for Enosis! Don't make me laugh! We should behave like Glyn, like Gloria, like the young people behind the "Diaspro Gallery", who are showing Angelos Makrides. Open galleries overnight, set up little publishing houses and convince the establishment not to buy yet another yacht or apartment in Limassol.'

Niki only half agreed with her sister: 'But we do belong to the Greek world. My mother comes from Macedonia, my father from Famagusta. I belong to a generation that has lived through extremes, right up close: from our grandmother at the spinning wheel to advanced technologies, from gypsies with dancing bears to the forerunners of computers. My six years in West Berlin left me pretty confused. I needed the scorching paralysing noon of Nicosia in the summer in order to remember who I am. I haven't opened a gallery, but I have opened a bookshop. "Kochlias", The Mussel. I wanted to have all the books which are important to me, around me. But –' she broke off and looked around the group – 'the circles here are small. It's sad but it's realistic: as a writer you're nothing if you aren't publishing your books with one of the big Athenian publishers.'

We all took a piece of the huge bass which Chrystalla had brought from the kitchen.

'Speaking of books,' continued Niki. 'You all know the story of my uncle Mitsos and the big library at his house in Famagusta, which has now been sealed up for over ten years. Recently I actually found, in a shabby antiques shop here – I can't really believe it – a few books from that library, a little battered and gnawed, but anyway. The dealer told me he has a middleman on the other side. The Turkish soldiers are flogging off books in a barracks behind the Castle at Kyrenia, not even by author or subject or date of publication, but by size and weight. There are piles of thick books, of medium-sized, and of thin, and that's how the price is set. Ten Turkish lira, five or two. You have a diplomatic passport,' Niki glared at me. 'Don't you think it's part of your duties to go check it out?'

I gave my most obedient nod.

Ioannis lit up a cigar. Outside a cicada was shrilling. Rita was prattling on mindlessly to herself about relatives and children.

'Politics isn't the only thing we should have banned,' Ioannis interrupted her. 'Rita, pack it in! No one's interested.'

'How have I put up with this man for a whole 32 years!'

'I want to go back to this theme of the periphery,' continued Ioannis, gently stroking his darkly gleaming skull. 'For me the margins are fun. The geographical, cultural stigmas associated with them are just talk. I really enjoy how the fiery temperament of the people here and their half archaic, half modern way of thinking form a beautiful unity. Why are we always looking to the West? Cyprus lies in the easternmost corner of the Mediterranean. The summit of Karpas points us to the Orient. It explains a lot: the hospitality, the sensuality, and also the lethargy of the Cypriots.'

Now Glyn piped up: 'For me everything in Cyprus is a crazy mish-mash, to speak only of the British, my compatriots, who were the last in a succession of twenty unfriendly colonisers stretched out over nine thousand years. They did a lot of crap, but you feel their influence everywhere, in the law system, the administration, the education system. They clamped down on the Oriental.'

'The British were in Syria and Palestine too. And what's left of them there?' countered Ioannis. 'The only Western constant in this part of the Mediterranean is Venice. I'll bet you anything that half of all the city gates, half of all the crumbling palaces and fortresses in this huge area have a winged lion on them. That's how it is and yet: what's left of Venice?'

He looked around the circle.

'A lot,' said Anna. 'A sense of scale and transience. A star from Venice encompasses our city. The Famagusta Gate has become a centre for the arts. Our lives would feel different if those buildings weren't there.'

'In the past, time is abolished,' said Niki. 'That's the key for me. The past, when it flourishes, is a beautiful counterweight to the ephemeral present. That's what I write about in my poems, and when I get one right, then I'm happy for an hour.'

Glyn nodded in agreement.

'Was that not a beautiful closing speech?' said Ioannis. He laid his cigar down on a plate, stood up and gave the signal for departure. In a short while the company were milling around in the entrance hall. I had brought my still half-filled glass with me and now I put it to my lips. I didn't want the evening to be over already. The people of Nicosia, even the artists, have the peculiar habit of arriving punctually, eating a great deal, and then saying their farewells straightaway after they've eaten.

'Do you want to leave me on my own so soon?' I cried out to the group.

They embraced me in sequence. Only Horst wanted to stay on, but Arianna dragged him away with her.

'The sun will be up soon,' she said, 'and I have to look after Eurydice. We have to shoot the video before it gets properly light.'

On Troodos: of the Archangel Michael, King Farouk and Arthur Rimbaud

With spring came the feeling that Cyprus is still a land of wonders. It was the flowers that did it, the flowers that shot up out of the barren earth, everywhere. Suddenly the entire island bloomed. There was the sea and there was the sea of blooms: poppy, yellow margue- rite, sweet pea, wild snapdragons, blue chicory, yarrow to head height, lining the roads. The blossoming of more than ten thousand cherry trees in the Marathasa Valley of the Troodos was announced around Nicosia as if it were a major political news story. The cherry blossoms of Mar- athasa were as famous as the pear harvest in Moutoullas a few months later.

So one Saturday in March we decided to go on a trip into the Troodos as far as Peristerona along the border. Then we walked in a wide arc into the folds of the great mountain, always climbing up to Kakopetria, where we ate a tea of pre- served fruits and listened to the noise of the wild streams.

The Troodos is massive and stately, the absolute opposite of the harsh, jagged, untamed Kyrenia Mountains. To the Kyrenia belong the Crusader castles, to the Troodos innu- merable churches and monasteries from the early Middle Ages. Crouched in neighbouring valleys or at the edge of a village, they seem unremarkable, most of them like small barns, with roofs that reach almost down to the ground. Art historians call them 'Barn Roof Churches' for this reason. Their origins reach back to the 10th and 11th centuries. Frightened by the constant threat of Arab attacks on the island, the Orthodox monks retreated into the pathless valleys of the Troodos, and many of the faithful went with them. When the Lusignans declared the Roman Church as the official religion and made life difficult for the Greek Orthodox Church, another wave of churches and monasteries was founded. These churches are not only difficult to find, they are also, except for special masses and anniversaries of saints, constantly closed, and it takes both time and trouble to find the village priest or to track down the key from the landlord of the nearest *kafeneion*. Almost all of these churches are entirely covered in frescoes, and put on a glorious display, unimaginably colourful, serious, fresh. They can give even the most rigorous atheist a lesson in fervour and piety.

We wanted to find two churches in particular on our way to Platres. One was 'Moni Panagias tou Arakou' in Lagoudera, of whose frescoes Niki talked constantly. 'The most expressive wall painting in the whole of Cyprus,' she said, 'created shortly after the Crusaders conquered the island.' I should look around the church carefully, she said. A hidden inscription refers to the year 1192. The frescoes were probably made by artists from Constantinople. All of which I forgot the moment I stepped into the church, overwhelmed by the luminosity of the colours, the dynamism of the figures and the audacity of the image-making, which seemed to me exceptionally modern. Here were white instruments of torture scattered across a ground of deep black; there Mary was lodged after the birth on a snow-white bed in the shape of a kidney, secured with double red straps and encircled by a black, jagged border. The most resonant for me were the frescoes on either side of the iconostasis, of two saints standing on tall columns. Each was enclosed by a grid-like net, drawn with touching delicacy, to prevent him falling from a great height. They awoke memories of my visit to the Basilica of Saint Simeon near Aleppo, and of all the stylites in the Syrian desert, men so renowned that a tremendous number of admirers visited them every day.

The unending white foam of blossoms, which awaited us in the Marathasa Valley, heightened the sense of exultation we had gained from our visit to the church in Lagoudera. Our eyes greeted the whiteness, flaring in the windswept sun, as if it were a purification. The light trembled in waves back and forth between the lush green earth and the white crowns of the trees. In Pedoulas, at the upper end of the valley, the gable-roofed Church of the Archangel Michael, the other church I absolutely wanted to see, was waiting for us. The painting here was more naïve, heftier. In the church in Lagoudera, all was spirit; spirit-apse, spirit-transepts. Here, by contrast, there was a great feeling of gravity. The Archangel himself was terrifically rendered, larger than life-size, with half-opened wings – we could almost hear them swishing. His serious, inward-looking countenance contrasted wonderfully with his plump angel's calves, stuck into mighty, colourfully embroidered boots. We could look at him again on the opposite wall, riding a cherry-blossom-white horse. His red lance was apparently so heavy that a gnome, sat behind him on the horse as if on a Vespa, was helping him carry the monstrous weapon. Over the north door a man surrounded by his family was presenting a model of the church to the Archangel. The garments of the women were covered in embroidery, like those you would still find today in Lefkara or the bazaar in Nicosia. But that wasn't everything. There were apostles, Marys, angels, devils and an abundance of saints, and yet this whirling fullness chased away earthly weight, so that here too every tiny detail of expression, of posture, of garment led directly to a core experience, an unwavering knowledge, that there is, within this world, a world beyond.

We arrived at Platres in the evening. I wanted without fail to spend one night in the legendary Forest Park Hotel, which had been erected in 1936 by a wealthy Greek as a luxury hotel in the Art Deco style. In the middle of an unendingly quiet, aromatic pine forest, it revealed its extravagant architecture, thrusting its giant prow, tiered over three storeys, above the crowns of the trees. In the lavish foyer, photographs in thin gold frames attested to the grand history of the hotel. One picture recorded its inauguration in June 1936. The British Governor of the time, Sir Herbert Richmond Palmer, stands on the entrance steps surrounded by officers. He is wearing a black armband. The caption explained: 'As a demonstration of grief over the death of King George V of England.' In another photo we saw the writer Daphne du Maurier, with an addition in her own hand: 'We have spent four happy, peaceful weeks here.' And in another, dated 1962, we could see Archbishop Makarios with Princess Irene of Greece. The most splendid picture, however, showed Farouk, the last king of Egypt, with his sheepdog. His ringed hand rests on the dog's neck, his eyes have the same pomaded sheen as his tightly combed-back hair. Farouk was so besotted with Platres that he had his own villa built here. Until it was completed he lived at the Forest Park Hotel, in 1946 and again in 1948, with servants, wives and dogs. It is alleged that Farouk invented the Brandy Sour, the Cypriots' national cocktail. The king had it mixed, they say, because as a Muslim he was forbidden alcohol and the drink looked like iced tea.

The hotel was still in family ownership. When we arrived, two men, young no longer, were shuffling around, both with prominent noses, both with strikingly large earlobes, thick with fur. One of the two led us around and proudly showed us the photographs and the plans of the architect Skyanides, who had built the hotel. Though the great days of the hotel were unquestionably past, a certain style was preserved in everything they did. Not only the crockery but also the tablecloths bore the hotel's emblem, a springbok standing on a rocky outcrop against a green shield. Above this shield a fantastical three-pointed crown was affixed, in the same reddish tone as the springbok.

We walked out of the foyer onto the spacious terrace. It was so enchanting that we no longer had any sense of the hotel's straining to demonstrate its dignity in decline. Here, except for the rustling of the trees and the singing of the birds, the quiet was absolute. George Seferis, one of the great poets, had memorialised the song of Platre's night-ingales in a poem. Now I could not stop myself thinking of him, the Greek diplomat, poet, friend of Henry Miller and Lawrence Durrell. He suffered all his life in the self-punishing conflict between his loyalty to the ever-chang-ing governments of Greece and his desire for freedom, for inward autonomy. Was it not similar for me? Didn't I want to have all my time to write? Free from the tedious reports to the 'office', free from the hierarchy of the ministry, free from the diplomatic skirmishing in Nicosia? 'You have to become a mummy to endure it all ...' wrote Seferis in his notebook. He had elevated his journey to Cyprus into a symbolic return to a visionary, spiritual Greece, in which the world of Homer still lived. I understood that and yet I could not follow him on his journey, however much I might wish for it. For that, I would have had to be Greek myself.

The dining room was only sparsely populated. It was still early in the season. Two older couples were sitting at a table and switching from Greek to English and back again. The two brothers took their meals here as well and bossed the waiters around gratuitously. The following morning the younger of the two was parading back and forth in front of the breakfast buffet in a pink Lacoste T-shirt. He greeted us friendlily and informed us without any segue that he was driving to Nicosia for the 'Oldtimer Rally' in his old Jaguar – *décapotable*, he said, spouting a smug, somewhat bruised French. We wished him luck and success and told him that we too would be driving back to Nicosia in a few hours, but we first wanted to have a look at Troodos itself, almost the highest point of the entire massif and also the summer residence of the British governor.

In the spring of 1880, Arthur Rimbaud had taken part in the building of this residence, at least until he had had to flee the island in a hurry following an argument with the paymaster and the executive engineer. Almost 70 years later the British Governor, one Lord Winster, had had a plaque affixed to the residence, with a text, curiously enough, in French: '*Arthur Rimbaud, Poète et génie français, au mépris de sa renommée contribua de ses propres mains à la construction de cette maison, MCCCCLXXXI*'. In other words: 'Arthur Rimbaud, poet and French genius, having no regard for his fame, contributed with his own hands to the building of this mansion.' They slipped up slightly with the date: it was 1880, not 1881. On 23 May 1880 Rimbaud reported the following to his family in Charleville: 'I found no work in Egypt and have travelled to Cyprus ... After a week I found the position which I still hold. I am a supervisor at the palace, which is being erected for the Governor-General on the summit of Troodos, the highest mountain in Cyprus (2,100 metres).' The tone of the letter is awkward, to say the least, and you can feel that Rimbaud considers this a chore – how tedious it is, writing to relatives. There is no trace of the meteoric poet. Only at the conclusion of the letter, after some moaning about the poor pay, does he become more personal: 'I am not well, I have heart palpitations, which are bothering me greatly. But it's better if I don't think of it. What else can I do? Besides the air here is very healthy. On the mountain there are only firs and ferns.'

The children were entirely indifferent to the French

genius, and to the British colonial residence. They chased a small black snake, which slid over the needle-covered ground and paused when the two of them could not follow it.

'I don't want to go back to Nicosia!' said Andrea in a firm voice. But in the car they fell asleep straightaway and had to be shaken awake when we got back to Gladstonos Street.

Of the silkworms in Lapithos

For us, the summer now had a name: Lapithos. At the beginning of July we migrated again and took possession of our beloved Harrison House. A cautious, happy ritual. I hung a wreath of garlic on a rusty nail in the kitchen. Anna and Andrea spread out their boxes of watercolours on the wooden table under the round arches. We greeted the palms, the jacaranda tree, the pepper tree, and the goldfish in the pond, which Orhan the gardener must have been feeding faithfully, as they seemed to us fatter and glossier than last year. The pert yellow of the lemons was close, and you could grasp the blue of the sea from the loggia. The wind from the dark mountains stirred the bright green leaves of the jasmine. Their shadows dappled the warm stony ground. All was good.

Early that evening we went shopping at the *bakkal*, where we were embraced as old friends. Karin inspected the aubergines, the plump broad beans, the leaves of wild dandelion.

'Those will make a delicious salad this evening!' she announced.

We bought bread and butter and sheep's cheese. The yoghurt was sold in round earthenware vessels. The clay draws out the water. Cypriot wine may not be, but Cypriot yoghurt is the best in the world. Punctually, during supper, the two geckos appeared. They paid no heed to us. Yet I, well laden with Lal, experienced their zig-zag hunt across the face of the wall as a gesture of welcome.

The following morning, after breakfast, we walked to the sea. A small restaurant had opened on a rocky plateau directly beneath Lapithos. Everything was very makeshift: a few wobbly tables and wicker chairs, a flimsy wooden fence around and an awning overhead. It was lovely after a swim to drink one more *cay* in the shade and look out over the water. The air was so clear, as palpable as it had been before on the beach at Salamis, an immaterial substance. It tolled softly, and I could almost hear ringing, had there not been waves beating against the rocks below, sending up a deep gurgling.

For the first few days we moved within a narrow radius, in the inner courtyard of the house and on this beach, which had remained entirely rustic. Some sheep romped about right up to the rocks on the water's edge. One midday, on the next finger of land, a dozen black donkeys stood under a mulberry tree. They were avoiding the sun and had thrust their noses into the dense shade near to its trunk, so that only their black hindquarters could be seen. The effect was of a bar with a dark green roof, mobbed by thin-legged men.

Little by little we ventured further, drove to Kyrenia and Bellapais or to the Moon Beach, even though we dreaded the long march across the glowing sand. The churches of Lambousa were still behind the military cordon. One evening Karin said that we finally had to conquer our beautiful lethargy and drive to Soli and Vouni, via Morphou. She was keen to play the archaeologist, as before at Salamis.

Morphou turned out to be a boring, small provincial town. It was, however, to a far greater extent than Lapithos, a centre for lemon and orange plantations. They grow bananas and vegetables there as well, but it was the smell of the citrus fruit that wafted invigoratingly through the streets. The Lusignans had pushed to develop the agriculture on the fertile plain of Morphou, then mostly cotton and sugar cane. Copper and iron ore mining had also played a major role here for centuries. Immediately next to the fields of ruins at Soli, the rusty remains of a conveyor loomed up into the sky alongside a cable car with seized up, rust-red ore buckets running down to a dilapidated roadstead on the coast. Our compensation for this view of ugly industrial buildings was the spectacular remains of an amphitheatre and a temple of Aphrodite. Soli, like Paphos, had been one of the island's great royal cities in the 6th century before Christ. Herodotus mentions it and Strabo traces the name back to the philosopher Solon, who advised King Philokypros to found a city there. We burrowed. A marble frieze from the baths, decorated with stylised flowers, was too heavy to drag back to the car. We found glazed black potsherds and remnants of ancient glass. Suddenly a gaunt, bark-brown man appeared in front of us. He was wearing a felt shawl of the kind the shepherds here drape over their shoulders. A short black beard framed his heavily lined face.

'*Hayir!*' he shouted excitedly. 'No, no! Forbidden!' His tone was threatening. He pulled a biro out of his threadbare trousers and noted down our car registration number on the back of his hand. We remained relaxed. After all, we hadn't pulled the Venus of Soli out of the earth. She was standing in the museum at Nicosia. Not even a marble knee or a silver coin. I tried to calm the man, but without success. Later, in the car on the way to Vouni nearby, I said that in the first moment, when the man was reaching into his pocket, I had hoped that he was about to pull out a cloth, unfold it and offer us a few gems for sale, an Artemis cut from bright red carnelian for example, or Eros on a dolphin.

'You dreamer,' said Karin. 'Of course that's what you thought. And with a gem like that you would have had a beautiful ring made for me straightaway.'

The palace at Vouni, situated on the peak of the mountain nearby and built long ago to control Greek-friendly Soli, proved to be heavily ruined. Of the once magnificent castle with more than 120 rooms, only the foundations remained to be seen. But the view from the site encompassed the entire sparkling bay of Morphou. This bay is wide enough to fit in the Greek, Phoenician and Persian navies all at once, I thought to myself.

Late in the afternoon, when we returned to Lapithos, tired and covered in dust with a few small pieces of mosaic, sherds and fragments of glass in our pockets, Mark was standing outside the door. He wanted to see how we were getting on. And he wanted especially to introduce me to the old, now retired teacher in Lapithos: 'He knew my father well. And his son has just set up a silkworm farm in Lapithos. You have to take a look. The son, his name's Rauf, was inspired by an old, buried tradition of the village, which he aims to revive.'

So it was that, in the midst of our summer at Lapithos, I experienced something I will never be able to forget: the noise at Rauf's worm farm, which filled the whole, large space. It was an old, abandoned agricultural building, probably of Greek ownership. Here Rauf had set up his racks. The cultivation crates extended up to the ceiling in multiple layers. Each individual sheet was thickly covered with freshly plucked mulberry leaves. You didn't see the worms. You heard them. Silkworms are pale and plump but small, and their mouthparts are smaller still. The chomping of one worm on a leaf you can't hear. But here in this hall, umpteen thousand silkworms were at work, and I heard their nibbling, chomping, gobbling and devouring umpteen thousand times over. It is not an easy noise to describe. It was like an unswerving, unrelenting scraping and burrowing, a soft, never-ceasing gentle rustling, a blind voraciousness, densely filling every last corner of that vast factory, as if something was at work, something stronger than us.

Rauf was full of his plans.

'Pupation begins in a month's time,' he said. 'It's hard to imagine, but these larvae produce a thread from their lower mouthparts which can be up to four thousand metres long and starts to set immediately on contact with air. The larvae make their cocoon out of this thread. But we destroy this pupal peace and kill the cocoon before the moth hatches out. We throw it into boiling water and then unwind the silk thread. The women of Lapithos will weave fantastic fabric,' he sighed happily. 'It is all just a question of time. It has already begun.

'You must come when we throw the pupae into the hot water. They hiss and jump about like popcorn, honestly! It's as if they're alive, though in fact they've long since been strangled by their own silk thread. We reel that thread onto little sticks and collect it up.'

'And the grubs?'

'We give the grubs to the chickens. Or we use them as bait when we go fishing.'

The same afternoon Rauf took me to meet his father Nâzım, who had taught classes in Lapithos under the English and had been the only Turkish Cypriot at the teacher training college. He spoke perfect English and, as he later assured me, perfect Greek too. An amiable, already half dried-out little man, he led me straightaway into his parlour, gave me a *kahve* and began without preamble to talk about Austen Harrison.

After Sir Austen had taken possession of his summer house – 'Don't you love it?' he interrupted himself. 'Doesn't it radiate humanity of scale, a great harmony?' – he had wanted to find out everything about Lapithos and along the way, learn a little Turkish. Nâzım seemed destined for the role. He had been born in Lapithos, studied briefly in England, and then lived in Kyrenia before he soon returned to Lapithos.

'Ah, love!' he said, rapping his little stick against the floor and glancing over at the photo of a young woman, which stood framed on a shelf among trinkets and books and next to a sofa covered with a throw of green satin, drooping down on all sides.

He returned to his thread: 'This town has changed a great deal, especially since 1974. The churches have been plundered. All the Greeks, including even my colleagues at the school, of whom I was very fond, were expelled and forced to head south. And as a result the Anatolians came, uncouth people, who don't suit Cyprus.'

After a pause he said: 'It's good that Sir Austen didn't live to see it. He loved Cyprus. But his heart remained in the Middle East. I don't know how much you know about him, but his greatest time as an architect was in Jerusalem. Do you know the Archaeological Museum there, opposite the King David Hotel?'

He leapt out of his chair and fetched me a photograph of the museum.

'Sir Austen built that. Together with Eric Gill, the famous British graphic artist and designer, who designed the decoration over the entrance. Austen considered it his masterpiece.'

The picture showed an unusually forceful building, an amalgam – if such a thing can exist at all – of British, Ottoman and desert architecture. With thick walls, built entirely of bright yellow sandstone, it was dominated by a tower which could even have been the fat ziggurat of a central Asian temple.

'It exudes self-confidence,' I said, 'and it seems to fit in in Jerusalem.'

'Sir Austen talked a great deal of his time in Palestine, where he was Chief Architect from 1923 to 1937, I think. There were many finds from antiquity in his house, which he had brought with him from Palestine. He was a collector, you know. Sculpture, amphorae, superb icons, as well as pictures by his British painter friends. He loved those things. And almost more than that, he loved playing the host. Many people dropped by. Lawrence Durrell, of course. Alfred Perlès. Freya Stark. Do you know her? A wonderful travel writer. Iraq, Yemen, Hadhramaut. The gates to the Orient.'

Nâzım told his stories well. With each additional sentence this character – who really I only knew from the dish as a prancing architect – gained new features, sharper lines. And I realised something else during our conversation: that his house, Harrison's House, had imposed itself upon me as a criterion against which I valued and measured the mountains, the gardens, the honey-yellow Abbey and the other houses.

We passed through the summer and the summer passed through us. They were happy days. I met with Nâzım a few more times. The girls asked when the next circumcision celebration was. Our neighbour, the 'inspector from the mainland' invited us for *meze*. The early morning was always the most beautiful time. The mountains were still black silhouettes against an absolute green silence. Then the sun came and the slime trails of the snails on the stone tiles began to glisten like silver decorations.

One midday at the end of August, Mark knocked on the door. He had spent part of the summer in England. He looked nervous. After the second rakı he came clean. He had money troubles. There was an inheritance dispute in England. The lawyer was bloody expensive.

'I have to sell this house,' he said, 'no matter how difficult that is for me. I have the feeling that you are happy here. Wouldn't you like to buy it?'

We looked at him, dumbfounded.

'I've spoken with an agent in Kyrenia, a British guy who knows the area well. The price is £66,000. It's a lot, but then again, it's not a lot – for the most beautiful house in the Eastern Mediterranean.'

He was quoting Durrell. We nodded. We asked for time to think. We had three restless days and three sleepless nights. We considered how we could finance it. Jointly with friends? Wouldn't we be binding ourselves too much to one place? Would the journey here via Istanbul or Mersin – when I was no longer working in Cyprus and no longer had a special passport – become too troublesome?

'Think it over,' said Mark. 'One important point. This house is not a Greek possession. In the land register at Kyrenia it's listed as foreign-owned. In that sense there's no problem with international law.'

In the end we decided not to buy. From then on we looked at the terrace with its arcade, the great hall, the garden, the goldfish and the lemon grove as though for the last time. Can there be so many last looks? Two days before we moved back to Nicosia we drove one more time to the Moon Beach. I was careless and stretched my feet out of the shadow from the sun umbrella and into the sun. That evening the tops of my feet were swollen and purple. They ached. My toes looked like little magnolia buds, my insteps like two large, oblong puffballs, which, if you stepped on them, would burst and send swirls of poisonous red dust into the air. This burning was a portent. That's how I saw it. My punishment for rejecting the Harrison House.

A Byzantine excursion

To remember was misery. For the Greek Cypriots the North was the lost country. They invoked the name of Karpas with particular melancholy. It had been a Greek heartland, with the pilgrimage monastery of Saint Andreas right at the tip of that ever-tapering, 80-kilometre-long promontory. In 1975 some Greeks had refused so furiously to be part of the move south that in the end the authorities had felt powerless against them and from then on a handful of UN soldiers had taken responsibility for the safety of the holdouts. These Greeks still live in Rizokarpaso, the main town on the peninsula, and in a few villages around it, growing ever older and dying. Their children and children's children have for a long time lived in the Greek part of the island, primarily for the sake of the schools. Turks from the mainland have moved in, but Karpas remains thinly populated, as it was before. Driving through the undisturbed landscape, it was hard to imagine that in Byzantine times here there had been one village, town, church or monastery after another. The real target of our journey was the church of Saint Philon.

We had driven past Famagusta and then across the Mesaoria plain – which now in autumn, after the long summer, stretched yellow and parched down to the sea. The mountains were far away. Troodos lay behind us; the Kyrenia

Mountains were a blue-black strip running along beside us to our left. Small white clouds splashed small black shadows across the yellow plain. Beyond Famagusta, beyond Salamis, by the last foothills of the Kyrenia, began Karpas.

We made our first stop near the village of Sipahi, at the ruins of the early Christian basilica, Agía Trías. There wasn't much to see, some foundation walls and mosaic floors. Two kids who were playing in the ruins led us to some unusual mosaics in an apsidiole. One of these mosaics depicted two sandals, with black soles and bold red straps. When one boy poured water from his plastic bottle onto the mosaic, these straps lit up powerfully. They became symbols of the still living practice of pilgrimage.

From Agía Trías it was not far to Agios Philon. This well-preserved church, stood at the sea's edge, captivated us instantly. Was it the location? The colour of the stone, a dark honeycomb-yellow? The three tall, supremely elegant fan palms, shaking themselves out over the church in the sea breeze? Or was it the architecture, graceful, essentially modest and yet full of subtle detail?

We swam between the rocks below the church, and as we swam we kept on looking back up at it, enchanted, magically attracted, as if by a miracle, how it stood entirely alone in this empty place and yet had defied every hatred, every stroke of fate.

Aféndrika, a ruined Byzantine town of several houses, churches and warehouses about seven kilometres away from Agios Philon, seemed to us even more abandoned. As we approached, dozens of lizards ran off in all directions. Then we came across a black snake, almost two metres long and as thick as a garden hose. It was sunbathing, perpendicular, on the outside wall of a shattered basilica. When it heard our steps, it rolled and meandered away. There were no people, no inhabited buildings in sight, except one lone shepherd in the distance crossing a field of blue thistles.

'I feel like time has stopped,' said Anna, our little philosopher.

We got to Rizokarpaso in the early evening. The place seemed to have no actual centre. It was frayed, as if every house insisted on its own garden and its field of vegetables and would have nothing to do with its neighbours. The old Greek gymnasium was enthroned on a hill, a Parthenon in miniature. The mosques yielded little, the churches were barricaded and seemed to turn us away. A few empty, very stately houses featured ornamented borders over their entrances in an archaic style, which I had seen nowhere else on Cyprus. Next to the little hotel where we had taken rooms, a good-looking young man tried to flog us a couple of dusty kelims.

'How are you today?' he asked, and immediately answered himself with a smile: 'Me, not so good.'

We inspected his merchandise over a glass of tea until our host fetched us and took us over to a covered table on the hotel verandah. He tried to tell us about the unusual features of Karpas but we didn't get far. He changed the subject and told us that he came from Paphos and that he still had a 'cup of longing' for Paphos. But – he opened his arms and turned through a complete circle – this Karpas is beautiful. A miracle of nature. Yes, a miracle of nature, he repeated, and as a tribute to nature he opened a bottle of white, 'Villa Doluca'. We sat on the balcony wreathed in brown vine leaves in front of his shabby hotel, the Pension Sunset, and made plans for the next day.

'You have to go to the Golden Beach,' he said. 'It has the clearest water. Like in the Caribbean,' he added emphatically, as if he had been to Martinique or Cuba dozens of times. From him we finally learnt that the area around the monastery of Saint Andreas was a military restricted zone, to which you could only gain access on the main Christian holidays – 'and with three stamps'.

As our dessert of chopped-up slices of dripping watermelon arrived, the Pension lived up to its name. The sun slid away and dropped behind the palm. Darkness fell.

Next morning we drove past cornfields and cypress groves, past mighty carob trees and endless rows of age-old olive trees to the beach our host had so fiercely praised. We stopped just once, in a village with a squat old Greek church. The nave was completely empty and had been used as a stall; parallel with it ran a narthex whose roof was held up by stout white columns. The master builder had used Roman capitals as pedestals for the columns. This example of the long tradition of architectural recycling, so commonplace across the Eastern Mediterranean, touched me. Where did these capitals of white marble, far more elegant than the church itself, originate? Were they brought here from Salamis at the behest of some local prince of the church? The village gave no answer. Nothing stirred. It was all so peaceful that if you didn't know anything about the history of Cyprus, you might have thought that these were the happiest people, people who had slipped through history's net, evaded its grasp.

Our host had not overpromised. The water at the 'Golden Beach' was clear to the bottom. The shadows of the clouds wandered over the white dunes. We swam and paddled around in the water until we could do so no longer. Back in Nicosia I still sensed the wet air on my face, saw in front of me the translucent, blistering foam, which sank, hissing quietly, into the sand, the waves, which grabbed at our feet, felt still the two currents when I was standing in the water up to my shoulders, one going past my chest and back towards the beach, the other, deeper, passing my legs towards the open sea, that glittering surface, on that day more white than blue, reaching to the horizon. The waves flickered like graphs on an immeasurably vast, divine video screen.

We ate red mullet, deliciously fresh, in a wooden hut at the seam between dunes and maquis.

'Why don't we stay here?' Andrea began her regular lament. 'I don't miss Nicosia. Not even school.'

'And it doesn't miss you either,' added Anna mischievously. 'Let's hire a tent! We can do something like that here, can't we?'

The geckos of Bellapais

The house I rented for my third and final summer on Cyprus bore no comparison to the Harrison House. I had found it in a newspaper advertisement. It belonged to an old lady in London who had arranged for an agent in Kyrenia to transact all her business. As it was shaded by a massive walnut tree, it was called Walnut Cottage. It stood by a ravine in Bellapais, halfway between the Abbey and Lawrence Durrell's house up the hill. When I inspected the property with the agent, Selim Bey, I was at first almost repelled. It was three narrow storeys high, had low ceilings, and you could only catch a snippet of the sea from the top floor. Behind the house, clinging to the slope, there was a deep-set terrace, a sort of stony hollow, and behind that not really a garden, but more an expanse of sloping earth containing fruit trees and unkempt geranium bushes. Three old copies of the *Guardian* from last year lay on a chair in one of the bedrooms. On the bookshelf a few tattered novels were sleeping, alongside Durrell's book about Corfu, its binding spoilt by damp. I was on the point of rejecting Walnut Cottage when – on the little square in front of the Abbey, underneath the Tree of Idleness, with the beauty of the Gothic cloister behind me – the place started to work its charm on me again. The house was measly compared to the Harrison House, but wasn't Bellapais more beautiful than Lapithos? In the end I signed the tenant's agreement in Selim's office and when summer came, at the end of June, we installed ourselves in Walnut Cottage.

On the other side of the small ravine stood two ruined houses of commanding proportions. They must have belonged to Greeks. On the first night she spent in Bellapais, Karin was woken by long, deep cries and wild moans coming from one of these houses.

'These Turks are real lovers!' she blurted out.

It was only the following morning that we found out that the ground floor of one of the two houses was used as a stable. Billy goats were romping about by the fence, which enclosed the entrance. It must have been their heartrending cries, when they mounted the nanny goats.

It was a hot summer. We spent most of the time naked in the stony hollow, spraying each other with the garden hose. The children found a chameleon in the reeds, which grew high out of the ravine in front of the house. This animal, entirely green amongst the green reeds, fascinated them, particularly its little toes, which clasped the shrubbery affectionately, and even more its yellow pinhead eyes on their wrinkly green inverted cones, which rotated independently of each other, scanning the world.

Despite the dense leaf canopy of the walnut tree, the light blazed everywhere. In the mornings everything – the stones, our skin – heated up very quickly in the sun. The light bit into our eyes. I pruned dried-out geranium leaves, Karin read, and Anna and Andrea dismantled the summer on the stone wall: cypress cones, beetle cases, dried-out thistle flowers, antennae and wings of butterflies, leftover yellow needles. Sometimes we heard the bells of the she-goats in the abandoned Greek house. Sometimes a ginger striped tomcat visited. The name we gave him – Nero – didn't entirely suit his languid yawn. When twilight passed his cat's eyes, a wind grazed down the mountains and slowly moved the walnut leaves. A constant, buzzing noise. In those July days it was the mountains that most enchanted me.

Unlike Lapithos, which lay on the foothills in front of the mountains, in Bellapais the rocks soared into the sky directly behind the village. Over the course of a day the mountain range was constantly changing its colour and shape. In the morning, backlit, it was grey and limpid; by midday it was green with the coruscating pine forests clinging to its steep slopes. In the afternoon this succulent green blended – passing along a subtle scale of colours – little by little into a dark, replete, green-brown. Yet it was only in the evening that the mountain range revealed its full, tiered and jagged majesty, as if a giant had unfolded a pop-up chain of purple mountains, which slowly sank into a deep blue and then an ultramarine, then almost black. The spectacle had theatrical qualities. Add in the three Crusader castles and you felt as if you were on the forestage of a gigantic open-air opera, which had to begin any minute now, with hunting calls, the tumult of battle or lovers' oaths. But nothing happened. The mountains kept their absolute silence.

This nightly show had many nuances. Sometimes the sky stayed white for a long time, while there were shades of orange or scattered crystals of brown at the lower levels of the mountains. It was a constantly renewed collaboration between sea and moon, clouds and humidity. Once, when the highest peaks of the mountains were glowing red, I was reminded of the lines of the great Costas Montis:

Twilight arrived
With two pairs of red cherries in her ears,
With a white paper screen
Over the mountains of Kyrenia.

I had formed the habit, in early evening, at the aperitif hour, of ambling down to the Tree of Idleness and drinking a Brandy Sour there. Little by little I got to know some of the villagers. The café owner was old. Perhaps at the beginning of the fifties he had known Lawrence Durrell? Perhaps his father had been the proprietor of the café then? His English was so bad that we could discuss only the most lapidary matters.

'Brandy Sour okay?'

'Yes, good, very strong.'

Pause.

'Did you know Lawrence Durrell?'

'Daril?'

'The guy of the *Bitter Lemons. Acı Limonlar*?' I gestured towards the mountains.

'Yes. Yes. *Acı Limonlar*.'

The Brandy Sour really was good, and strong. Of all the visitors to the café, the amiable Uzun spoke the best English. He was a PE teacher and a beekeeper in his free time. His hives, as he explained to me, stood in a clearing about three hundred metres above Bellapais. He caressed a black cat, which was nuzzling the leg of our table.

'Do you know why I like cats?' he said. 'Cats eat lizards, which would otherwise eat my bees. The cats do well. They feed themselves on lizards and snakes.'

'There are plenty of snakes then?'

'Sure. But mostly just the black vipers. They're not poisonous.'

Uzun desperately wanted to show me his clearing. But my curiosity about swarms of industrious bees had its limits.

'Let's wait a bit,' I said. 'I have a lot to write and to read. We'll meet here again tomorrow, at the Tree of Idleness.'

When I got home, I could no longer find my poetry notes. Since I had been living in Bellapais, I seemed to have fallen into a system of heightened centrifugal force. Sunglasses, driver's licence, snorkel, a slip of paper with important phone numbers and now even these scribblings had sought out some other orbit. I had forgotten Nicosia and a great deal else. When the children were asleep and Karin was in the hollow finishing off a novel, I tried to write at the simple table on the top storey. Every night the light from the standard lamp drew in the insects and so the geckos after them. The geckos' bodies were slimmer and more elegant than those in Lapithos. They were also more translucent. There was always a darkish lump in their middle, beneath their diaphanous skin. It was the flies and mosquitoes and baby praying mantises they had already eaten. I hoped that I'd be able to count the individual insects but it wasn't possible. They had already been mashed into a dark pulp by the stomach juices. The elegance of the Bellapais geckos extended into their toes, which were not the usual, rather ugly broad ones. It was the ridges on these toes, equipped with tiny hooks, which allowed the lizards to scurry about on the ceiling or even on the windowpanes, like sleepwalkers, or else to wait and wait, stoically, until their prey appeared.

One night, as I was writing, a beetle on its back was giving out a desperate whirring. Immediately the smallest of the geckos got himself down onto the floor and devoured the beetle with a single gulp. Karin thought I was mad to believe that I could make friends with the geckos and to think that they recognised me each evening, as I recognised them. But once one of the lizards stopped on the wall, exactly at the height of the surface of the table and stretched out the toes of his left front leg towards me. A thin fan. I stretched out the fingers of my writing hand in answer. It was almost as if our two so different instruments of touch were making contact. Of this intimate moment, which was quickly over, I told Karin nothing.

With Uzun however, the following evening, Brandy Sour in hand, I turned the conversation to geckos and expressed the hope that no cat could ever eat 'my' geckos.

'*Tarentola mauritanica*,' he sighed. 'That's what they're called in the schoolbooks. They're part of the Mediterranean like olive trees and wine. There are so many of them. You really won't notice if a cat eats one of them.'

In spite of these cool observations Uzun was in a way even crazier than me. He went so far as to claim that the geckos had a 'loud voice'. I just had to listen carefully. Then he talked about the gecko's tail, which also has an adhesive mechanism. This was the part that the cats most prized. It was, apparently, the tastiest bit of a gecko.

Thank God that İzzet joined us and sat himself at our table. İzzet was the gardener who looked after the trees and plants around the Abbey. He was a mainland Turk, born in Mardin, had studied horticulture and the layout of Ottoman parks somewhere and then come to Cyprus in 1981. His family background was not exactly everyday. One grandmother was of Armenian ancestry; he had Coptic relatives in Alexandria. This bastardisation had made him into an alert young man, who knew his way around several cultures.

This evening he was agitated as he thought that the 'great Coptic storm-winds' were about to hit us, earlier than usual in the year. They were strong, like the Mistral in Provence or the Tramontana in Italy, and they would last for three days solid. The most devastating was El Mickness, the 'Broom Storm', and then El Shams El Kebira, the 'Great Sun Storm'. He was afraid for his cypresses in the cloister and for some tall fan palms, flexible but still fragile, which stood on the slope directly below the refectory. We tried to calm him down. Uzun was of the opinion that these winds, notorious throughout the Eastern Mediterranean, never came before the end of the summer. I ordered İzzet an extra-strong Brandy Sour. The mountains were having their purple hour. On the little street with the Abbey complex along one side and several restaurants and shops along the other the villagers were by now promenading up and down, enjoying the vanishing of the sun, greeting each other, chatting and proudly showing off their little children.

I flattered myself that I could distinguish Turkish Cypriots from mainland Turks by their clothing, their gestures. But was there really such a thing as a 'Cypriot'? The Greek Cypriots say that they are descended from the Mycenaeans, as well as the Ptolemies and the Phoenicians. Their Greek is nearer to Homer's than the Greek that Athenians speak today. And the Turkish Cypriots hark back to the Ottomans. But who now can trace it all back, after 10, 12, 15 waves of occupation and as many colonial overlords, and so much ethnic and religious to-ing and fro-ing? While my thoughts were wandering, Uzun had got back onto his number one topic, the bees. But now Anna came running up, planted herself in front of our table and cried out with her blue eyes glittering: 'Swordfish in ten minutes!'

I took my leave of the bees and the Coptic winds, of my acquaintances, our host and the Tree of Idleness, and trotted off up the street with Anna to the mighty walnut tree.

We made a few excursions that summer. To Kyrenia, naturally; to the Moon Beach as well. To Orga, a no-horse town a few kilometres beyond Lapithos. And to the Antiphonitis Monastery, which I had not yet seen and which perched in the middle of the Kyrenia Mountains, on the way to Buffavento Castle. You could only get to the monastery along a narrow track, which led through fragrant pine forests and had stunning views out over the coastline and the sea from a great height. Wherever we stopped, the bed of needles on the ground was covered in cartridge cases of many colours. It must get pretty lively up there in hunting season. For two hours we had not seen another human being, so I was glad when we came across a custodian in front of the monastery, sat in front of a wooden shed, staring into space. We must have been the first visitors in days. He unlocked the church door for us excitedly.

Antiphonitis, large and squat, stood above a precipice. The clearing where it sat, a kind of green terrace, was not visible from the peaks above it. It seemed that, as elsewhere on the island, the monks had moved here to be safer from the Arab invaders and no doubt in later centuries the tax collectors for the Ottoman rulers had also struggled to find this hideaway. We stepped into the church as if into a mystical, inwardly directed world. The overwhelming force of this sacred building derived from this feeling and this feeling in turn stemmed from the architecture itself. Eight mighty, irregularly placed columns, covered over and over with frescoes, carried the round roof and the short nave. These frescoes continued onto the walls of the church in an ecstasy of angels and Church Fathers. The layers of colour were still so vivid that I assumed the many damaged sections could not have been caused by time and weather – nor could they be part of the devastation wrought by the Turkish soldiers, given that, as the custodian told us, the monastery had been declared a museum immediately after the invasion. But I was telling myself fairytales. A few weeks later, visiting the Byzantine Museum in Nicosia, I saw some fragments from frescoes, especially the faces of saints, which had originated at Antiphonitis and apparently had been won back by the Orthodox Church after a long legal battle.

We got to know Bellapais better that summer too. Our most beautiful discovery was the gardens directly below the mighty outer wall of the refectory. Here pomegranate and mirabelle trees, hibiscus and oleander, cypress and ancient palms formed a lush green thicket. Above them, the exterior wall of the Abbey, facing the sea, clearly divided by the six braces and six windows of the refectory, soared almost 40 metres into the sky, obscuring the Kyrenia Mountains, an austere, golden-brown assertion in the afternoon light. The white and grey doves launched themselves off the braces, much more slowly than the swallows, who sailed joyfully through the air, swerving madly.

August was half over before we knew it. I had travelled a few times to Nicosia to check everything was in order. Our friends – Niki, Horst, Arianna, George, Glyn – were all on the coast somewhere. I looked through the post at home and the cables at the embassy and then was quickly back in Bellapais. We had become accustomed to Walnut Cottage, but leaving there would feel easier than leaving the Harrison House the previous year.

At the café under the Tree of Idleness there were still a few more rounds of goodbyes. Karin came with me.

'To make an ending,' she said.

The old host on his way to serve his customers always took a detour past the chair where Karin was sitting. The sly old dog must have fallen in love with her shoulder blades.

In the café three antediluvian refrigerators muttered to themselves. I told Uzun about the development of my relationship with the geckos at the cottage.

'I've been watching them every night. It was always very quiet. But this "loud cry", which you made those claims about, I've never heard it. Once it did seem to me that the smallest of the geckos was whimpering, but it was a silent whimper. Or a feeble snort.'

'They only cry out when they're discontented,' said Uzun. 'All that means is that they feel damn good in your company.'

'I'll make a lizard dish before we go,' suggested Karin. 'Thigh of gecko with tomato mousse.'

İzzet and Uzun looked at me pityingly.

'I'm going to be relocated in the autumn,' I said. 'To Bonn. I can't believe that we won't be coming back to Cyprus, to Bellapais, to you.'

On my last night in Bellapais, before I fell asleep, I imagined the loneliness of the geckos in a world without insects. Then I was rowing a boat, which was full of ashes and slowly sinking. I was terribly agitated. Over and over I said to myself in my dream: but ash is light, the lightest thing in the world.

The return

Ignoring two brief visits, which don't really count, I hadn't been back to Cyprus for any real length of time until last year. Back in the middle of the eighties, I was able to sing the island's praises. Praises that I've recorded here. Now, more than a quarter-century later, will I be able to do the same? Will this be a report on a renewed affection? Or only a reflection on the old one, a memory?

These questions are troubling me, as, in May 2012, I land at Larnaka and, taking a six-lane motorway, which did not exist back then, through the same ungreen, mountainous, karst landscape, arrive after a short time at Nicosia. The final kilometres run through business parks of the kind I have seen before on the edges of Beirut or in southern California. I take a room at a hotel, which sits on the perimeter of the old city. My first walk takes me to Gladstonos Street. On the way I want to drink a *metrio*, but the Garden Café isn't there any more. Obeying an old habit, I step into the Cyprus Museum and look for the black Stone of Kouklia. It is no longer there. I walk through all the rooms again. I ask an attendant. He tells me that a few years earlier a museum was established in Kouklia, next to the Temple of Aphrodite, in part of the Lusignans' fort. The stone has been returned there, 'to its old place'.

'Then I must go to Kouklia,' I reply. Without asking

whether Konstantis is still working at the museum, I go on my way.

Our house on Gladstonos Street feels stony, stonier than it is in my memory at any rate. Have some of the mighty old thickly scaled palms, which I liked so much, been felled? In any event the owner – or perhaps a later tenant – has concreted over part of the garden behind the house, the part where the orange trees stood. I walk along the street, which has preserved its genteel character. It is still lined with old houses in the classical style. Some luxury apartments have been built on the former waste ground next to the Junior School, but not too high, and using tasteful materials, nothing objectionable. At the end of Gladstonos I cross the little river gully and eucalyptus grove and reach the Turkish kiosk where before we used to drink lemonade with Anna and Andrea. Bridge House rises up behind it, but the Bridge House Bookshop, where I bought so many dusty books – Malcolm Lowry, Seamus Heaney, Douglas Dunn, Sylvia Plath, the English editions of Seferis, Elytis and Costas Montis – is no more. A business selling motorbikes and tyres has moved in.

I make another detour past the state theatre and through the park to the old border at the Ledra Palace Hotel, which we passed hundreds of times between 1984 and 1986. Here everything has been preserved as if under a glass dome. The Ledra Palace Hotel, which was the only hotel in the area until 1964, became the headquarters of the UN ten years before the Turkish invasion, as the violent disputes between the two populations escalated. The pale blue flag flutters on the roof as it ever did. In almost 50 years there has been no real movement towards a solution of the Cyprus problem. Back in 1984 I heard straight from the mouth of a senior international official: 'The UN are fed up with Cyprus.' It may be a responsible job, monitoring the peace, but it can also be deathly boring. I watch some UN soldiers on the little balconies outside what had once been hotel rooms, reading the paper, listening to the radio or hanging out their damp underwear.

I pace down the long alley of blue jacaranda trees. Near the checkpoint, the shot-up, burnt-out house which the Greek Cypriots left untouched as a memorial to the horrors of the Turkish invasion, is still standing. Behind the Greek Cypriot border guards, set slightly back from the road, is the pretty pink villa which is the home of the Goethe Institute. It occurs to me that there are no cars coming by and that clearly this crossing is for pedestrians only. I talk with a border guard about it. The soldier, referring to a slip of paper, explains to me how to get to a vehicle crossing from here. He finishes his short speech with the words: 'And then you cross to the occupied areas.' Is that now just a formula, something he repeats day in day out, or is he thinking about what he's saying? Does an element of pain resonate in his words? I asked for the information because I want to hire a car in the days ahead and drive into the North.

This is perhaps the biggest change of all: on 23 April 2003, Rauf Denktaş unilaterally decreed the opening of the border. People are still puzzling over his motives. The economy in the North was in decline at the time. Denktaş may have hoped to attract the Greek population and especially the tourists from the South, who could have been spending some of their money in Kyrenia, Bellapais and Famagusta. In the first weeks after the opening, as you may have read in the newspapers at the time, there were vast columns of Greek Cypriot cars. Every expelled Greek wanted to see their home village and their property. And they brought vast picnic baskets with them – this was the rumour – because they disdained to give the Turkish restaurateurs and occupiers a single cent. As soon as this first wave was over, disappointment set in. The Greek Cypriots realised that nothing else was going to change, that they would never get their houses and plantations and small businesses back, not now and certainly not peacefully. A flood of lawsuits was unleashed, the majority of which remain unresolved. The rush subsided, soon became a trickle, and finally petered out completely. The Greeks' overwhelming longing had been deadened by the realisation that the *fait accompli* of the partition had become so solidified that it was better, and wiser too, to concentrate on life in the South.

I leave the Ledra Palace checkpoint behind me, this place of decommissioned memories. For me, the returnee, my key reference points are Gladstonos Street on the one hand and Lapithos and the Harrison House on the other. But I want to spend a couple more days in Nicosia. I phone Niki. Conveniently, it is the closing night of an exhibition of her pictures this evening. She picks me up at the hotel. The gallery – 'Aeschylus 38' – is in the old city, near to the

Armenian Church and the Pancypriot Gymnasium. That I should end up seeing Niki again in her image-world is a happy coincidence. She has hardly changed; her eyes are as intense and dark as ever, and her all-conquering smile and nimble speech are all bathed in Mediterranean serenity.

Red dots are stuck on the labels next to the oil paintings, watercolours and etchings. Niki is euphoric.

'I'm sold out!' she shouts, entirely forgetting her serenity. 'I can't believe it! I'm sold out!'

The watercolours from a trip to Tunis particularly attract me. I fall in love with *The Girl from Beirut*. This etching shows a young woman in traditional costume on a geometrically patterned divan. Niki has coloured the etching. The young woman is holding a round peacock fan in a bright pink hand. The deep blue and flashing green of the feathers catch my eye.

By another coincidence, on my first evening back in Cyprus after such a long time, there is also a 'Museums Night' taking place. We walk first from the gallery to the house of the dragoman, Hadjigeorgakis Kornesios. Built of local sandstone in 1780 it is the most significant surviving residence within the Venetian city walls. Outwardly monumental, its interior enchants with colonnades, lavish arcades, alcoves and richly painted wood panelling on the walls and ceilings. 'Dragoman of Cyprus' was the title of the governor appointed by the Sublime Porte in Istanbul. The Ottoman sultan always bestowed this important office on a Christian and Hadjigeorgakis Kornesios, a Greek of Orthodox faith, was Dragoman of Cyprus for nearly 30 years, from 1779 to 1809. In the inner courtyard of the residence, which is now a museum of the city's history, a concert has just taken place. The audience are strolling around animatedly under the round arches and palm trees. The wine is being served with cheese and fat, gleaming black olives.

From there we head over to the Cyprus Contemporary Art Museum. Here too the atmosphere is good. The young, often stylish Nicosians are sitting on the lawn, drinking and discussing. I want to see my favourite painters again, Adamantios Diamantis, Stass from Paphos and George Pol Georghiou, the best known of them all, who had his studio in Famagusta and died in 1972, two years before the island was divided. The pictures are, to my chagrin, miserably presented. A 'Cypriot Hang' seems to be a salon-style hang to the power of ten. The paintings are slaughtering each other. Only one work by Angelos Makrides, which I know well from before, makes some space for itself. A foil of dull tin covers a sheet of chipboard, leaving just the outline of the head and chest of a human form. Above the head the tin foil is perforated. The dotted lines, arranged into a semicircle, suggest a halo. The piece – entitled *White Saint* – is a Cypriot variant on *arte povera*. It plays with icon painting, reinterprets that tradition and refers, without being theatrical, to the troubles Cyprus has endured. I linger in front of it for a long time.

'Let's go over there,' says Niki. 'It's not so late.'

We wander up Ledra Street, cross the 'green line' with few formalities and then we are in the Turkish zone. Here everything is dark, as if life has already ended.

'I know a café called Sabor. They'll definitely still be serving.'

Niki shows me the outside of the great caravanserai, *Büyük Han*, shrouded in night, and then the *Bedestan*, which has just been restored. We look through the side-windows of the Saint Sophia Cathedral, the coronation church of the Lusignans, into the illuminated interior. This view from the darkness of the whitewashed, soaring, sacred space overwhelms me.

'You must come back tomorrow and definitely have a good look at the *Bedestan*, and the so-called Lusignan House, which isn't far from here, and especially the restored Arabahmet quarter. It's home to the most beautiful houses in old Nicosia.'

Sabor is indeed still open. From the tables outside you can see the apse of the cathedral and some medieval houses with black palm trees soaring over them. We order wine. Niki spots an acquaintance at a distant table.

'A good painter,' she tells me. 'Called Emin Çizenel.'

We move to his table. Emin's companion, it becomes immediately clear in our conversation, has just organised a poetry action, which took place in Nicosia last weekend. The two men speak with panache about the bureaucratic and organisational barriers they had to struggle against. Three hundred poems by three hundred poets, all on the theme – very broadly interpreted – of reconciliation, were to be dropped from a helicopter over both halves of the city. Neither the Greek not the Turkish side would agree to the helicopter flight. At which point they had turned to the UN.

'But they were even worse than the others: fixated on the status quo to the point of hysteria.'

In the end they ordered two moored balloons from Belgium, which got here at the very last minute.

A very neatly dressed girl comes up to our table, her face an oval harmony, her skin smooth and flawless, as it never will be again. Her eyes want to sell us a bouquet of roses, her last it seems. The roses are in full bloom. With the fist of her free hand she is vigorously, almost brutally, pressing each blossom together, as if she wants to make each one back into a bud by force. Emin takes pity on her, buys the bouquet and gives it to Niki.

'They could have been fresher,' he mutters.

Emin has a striking face. It reminds me of the countenance of a Roman emperor, the young Diocletian perhaps, or the German painter Hans Purrmann. With a keen hooked nose and taut cheeks, it is a forceful, ancient face. He tells me that he's working at the moment with the soot from candles, which he transfers directly onto the canvas. His project *Chosen Tree* originated in this way. In this cycle of pictures he makes one of the four cypresses in the cloister at Bellapais burst into flames. For him, it is a ritual act. The light of the burning Cypress resin corresponds to the burning desire to begin afresh.

'To find a new source,' he says.

Previously Emin was interested in public wells, of the kind you still find in every Cypriot village, though most are no longer in use, because the houses have since got a direct connection to the water supply. On the way back Niki tells me that she particularly likes Emin's well pictures. They are in an entirely immediate way about water, which bestows life, which flows through our memories and can wash everything away.

'Everything,' she says. 'Screams, tears, bloodstains, border walls. In a hidden way Emin is a political painter and very engaged. I'll show you a catalogue back at my house. In the past these wells were essential for life. Many people relied on them, came with their cans and buckets to fill up with water. Now the wells have another identity, but Emin manages to give an aura to those unadorned cubes of cement, those plain brass taps. When I first saw his well pictures, I felt as if I'd turned on the tap myself and was wet through to my bones.'

When we say our goodbyes in front of my hotel, Niki says that she'd like to throw a dinner party for me the next day.

'With our old friends. I'll try them. Let me surprise you.'

On the misery of division

'What a strange island this is, moored between Europe and Asia!' exclaims Garo, a little too theatrically. 'The Oriental influences were strong here. They've evaporated. The permissiveness, the gentle, feminine barbarism, which Aphrodite introduced to the island long ago, it's all vanished. What's left is Greek pride and shitty nationalism. Alas! We're moving through the scree of history. But who's interested in these strata from the distant past? Where are they useful now? In the work of artists perhaps? In our unconscious?' Garo sighs with relish. 'Psychic sediments?'

Niki has introduced Garo Farosyan to me, an Armenian businessman, a high aesthete and a patron of the arts. A foundation he set up supports music and visual arts on Cyprus. He is the only one of Niki's guests that I don't know. Seated around her festive, flower-bedecked table are Horst and Arianna, the indestructible Gloria, who in old age is still running her gallery, and Ruth, proprietress of a bookshop on Sofocleus Street called Moufflon, stuffed full of treasures. If you're interested in the history of Cyprus and the Levant, you'll find long out-of-print coffee-table books, precious first editions of British travel writers and even occasionally a book whose inside front cover bears Lawrence Durrell's Ex Libris, a highly stylised red griffin. Once again, Niki is a superb host. Yet for me the conversation quickly becomes a *déjà entendu*. Straightaway, as it did a quarter-century ago, all talk again revolves around the so-called 'Cyprus Problem'. Islands seem to promote navel-gazing. Thus I am immediately asked for my first impressions. Whether I have noticed any changes, good or bad.

This is only my second day, I reply. I need a little time. I'm absorbed in my personal memories. I want to stay three weeks on the island.

My friends won't let it go. The opening of the border, I say, obviously that's the biggest change.

'It's odd,' says Gloria. 'When we drive up into the North, we feel as if we're in exile. Disorientated. And yet it is our homeland. A homeland that's become alien, an alienated homeland.'

'It's a paradox,' says Garo. 'The open border has cemented the division.'

'How's that?' I ask. 'When I was living and working here, the division of the island was just ten years old, and the border was impermeable. Now, though it's almost impossible to believe it, 38 years have passed since the Turkish invasion. Can a hope not get that old?'

'The last major chance for a solution was the Annan Plan in 2004. We popped some champagne corks then. We fantasised. We wanted to set up caravans next to our old houses so that we could oversee the restoration work. But the referendum went the wrong way. The majority of Greek Cypriots voted against it. I'm pessimistic about the future of the island now. Very pessimistic. I can't foresee any reunification, no matter in what form.'

Arianna contradicts Garo: 'I still have hopes for a

confederation, a federal state. There are surprises in politics. Things happen which everyone thought were impossible.'

'I'm pessimistic because the number of native Turkish Cypriots, who were always a minority, is getting smaller and smaller. The Anatolians who've moved over here now have the say. And these people from the mainland – at a guess, around 130,000, which is half of all the Turks living on our island – clearly they can't have any memories at all from the time before the division, of mixed villages, of living together. How could they? They simply weren't there.'

'True,' says Arianna. 'But the people who do remember that time are dying out. I actually base my hopes on the generations on both sides who were born after the invasion, after 1974. Memories disturb. Memories can cripple us. These young people are not hemmed in by memories. And they speak a different language. Communication works differently for them. They are computer children. With them, cohabitation will be possible. They'll surprise the older generation.'

Now Horst, who is always pretty taciturn, takes the floor. In his view the opening of the border has accomplished something at least: it has made contact easier. There is a certain openness now. People approach each other, they speak with each other, the intellectuals and the artists especially. That is a positive, even if both sides, when they look into the past, fill most of their vision with the events in which they themselves were victims. There hasn't been a coming to terms with history in the German sense. Not yet.

Niki talks about Turkish-Cypriot friends who bring their children over the border to a school in the South because of the extreme nationalist emphasis in education at the schools in the North. The chair of the Turkish-Cypriot Writers' Guild teaches at a university nearby. Things are beginning to shift.

'Agreed,' says Garo. 'There are these small, heartening examples. But they do nothing to break this stalemate, sadly. I think the real victims, the really bereaved, are the Turkish Cypriots, most of whom were forced to move and are now being crushed by the majority from the Turkish mainland. When something bad happens, most of them will emigrate to England, to Canada. They're on the starting blocks already.'

'Pessimist!' everyone shouts.

'Wait a moment. You know that the head of your Orthodox Church wants to build a new cathedral in Nicosia? It's going to be huge. The towers alone will be 60 metres tall. I think he wants to entice the Turks with that. So that they'll come and stick a couple of minarets onto the towers!'

We all have to laugh hard at that, even Garo. I use the pause to ask him if he knows the Harrison House in Lapithos. He doesn't know it, but he has heard about it. A corrupt Turk, Aşil Nadir, bought it off the Istanbul industrialist Koç. This Aşil Nadir grabbed a great quantity of Greek property in the North. He has had to stand trial in London for a long list of shady dealings; it was in the papers.

We have just devoured the light-heavy dessert of meringue on peach ice cream with cream when Garo looks at his watch and asks whether we might not want to come to

Delikipos with him. There's an open-air concert in his olive grove. On impulse, Niki, Arianna and I take up his offer.

After about 20 kilometres on the motorway towards Limassol, Garo turns off to the right. A narrow, winding road leads us very quickly into a peaceful, seemingly untouched landscape. Hundred-year-old olive trees grow on Garo's estate. Roses have entwined around their trunks and got lost among their branches, blossoming pink among the silver-grey leaves. Next to a fenced-off pond about three hundred chairs sit on a perfectly shorn lawn in the oblique early evening light. Gradually the bourgeoisie from Nicosia and Limassol take their seats. As the music begins the frogs awake, one, two cicadas as well. I find their croaking and thrashing suit Rossini and Mahler very well.

After the concert I spot Lellos Demetriades among the guests. I'm overjoyed to see him again. He is quite unchanged, the same keen eyes, the roguish smile, the joy in spinning a pointed yarn. Only his moustache, once inky black, has greyed. We embrace. Then he says, first of all, that he is no longer Mayor of Nicosia and, second, that he was mayor for 30 years. I like, as I did before, his ironical and slightly abstracted quality. It's almost impossible to believe that he is 75 years old. As Niki and Arianna want to stay longer, I travel back to Nicosia with him in his hefty Mercedes.

On the way he tells me that he's working on a book.

'Not a memoir. More an account of my dealings with Mustafa Akıncı, you know, who used to be Mayor of Northern Nicosia. Only a few people know that we used to meet secretly to make progress with projects which were essential for the city as a whole. A joint sewerage system, for example.'

The car reaches the top of a hill, from which we can see the lights of Nicosia and the outline of the mountain ranges to the north, black against an electric blue sky. Very soon after the invasion, the Turkish soldiers laid out thousands upon thousands of red and white painted stones with painstaking attention to detail on the slope of the mountain in front of Kyrenia, to form a colossal Turkish flag. It was so huge that in the daytime you could make it out from the Greek half of Nicosia with the naked eye. Now I cannot believe my eyes. It seems that since then every stone has been 'paired' with a lightbulb. They are illuminated in phases: first the star, then – two seconds later – the crescent and then – another two seconds later – the outline of the entire flag in red. Disco-imperialism, the likes of which I have never seen anywhere, not even at the border between North and South Korea. Lellos notices my astonishment.

'You know the electricity in the North is supplied by us,' he says. 'By the Cypriot government. When this spectacle began they made a formal protest. They made a whole heap of démarches: you can't do something like this with "our" electricity. Then the answer came back from Denktaş: we're running it with a generator from one of our barracks. We're not using your electricity.' Lellos gives me a sidelong glance. We are entering the outskirts of Nicosia. 'It's stories like that that show you how mean and shabby the details of partition are. But I do believe in a reunification of the two halves. Still. It'll be the young people, who aren't weighed down by our vicious history. They'll make it work.'

Half of Lambousa

I say to myself: the beautiful thing about writing is to live through something again, to turn back the clock. Now I am turning back two clocks, as it were; I am moving back and forth between two planes of time with different tempos, the Cypriot past and the Cypriot present.

One great contrast with the past is that I am no longer living and working here on the island, living off her and with her. I have returned as a tourist. For the coming nights I have reserved a room at the Dome Hotel in Kyrenia. Before, in a place so close to Lapithos and the Harrison House or later Bellapais, I would have needed no accommodation. Now I am curious about this hotel, which was built in the British colonial period and which I have never visited. Lawrence Durrell described it very waspishly in his Cyprus book: 'Never has one seen such extraordinary human beings as those who inhabited the Dome Hotel; it was as if every forgotten Victorian *pension* between Folkestone and Scarborough had sent a representative to attend a world conference on longevity. The figures, the faces, the hats belonged to some disoriented world populated only by Bronx cartoonists; and nothing could convince one more easily that England was on its last legs than a glimpse of the wide range of crutches, trusses, trolleys, slings and breeches-buoys which alone enabled these weird survivals to emerge from their bedrooms and take the pale spring sunshine of the Kyrenia waterfront.' Well, that was 1955. Now it is more than half a century later and a hell of a lot has happened in-between: the end of British colonial rule, Cyprus's independence, the Turkish invasion and the division of the island. The hotel has been completely renovated by its Turkish management in the last ten years. I am excited.

Niki insists on driving me to Kyrenia. She says that I can easily hire a car there for my other excursions. And with a hire car from 'over there' I can drive back and forth between the two halves of the island. I have to pay a small sum at the border for Greek motor insurance, but that is the only formality.

On the drive to Kyrenia, Niki tells me about the Dome Hotel. Her family often used the Dome for daytrips, when they weren't holidaying at her grandfather's house or Uncle Mitsos's villa in Famagusta. She was a small girl then. She had great fun jumping into the sea from the concrete pier in front of the hotel. It was so different to Famagusta – there you waded slowly into the shallow water, with rippled white sand under your feet all the while, whereas here she was immediately enveloped by the deep, always gently surging sea. In April 2003, when the border, sealed for so long, was opened, she paid a visit to Famagusta on the very first day and then in the late afternoon, still on the same day, she went to the Dome Hotel at Kyrenia.

'You see,' she remembers, 'I walked out onto the hotel terrace and a young Turkish man was just then singing the song *Sympathy is what we need my friends.* The evening sunlight was gilding the tables, the crackling wicker chairs, even the hotel guests. Then the waiter arrived. He noticed I had tears in my eyes. That made him think. He murmured: "I'm from Rizokarpaso too." I didn't know what he meant by that. I said to him, I'd like an Alexander, and I thought back to those years when I was discovering young men and cocktails.'

Kyrenia too has suburbs that are new to me. But we quickly get to the still familiar old city and the harbour. As we are walking along the high white corridor from the reception of the Dome Hotel to the terrace, the door of a conference room opens. A placard next to the door reads: 'Meeting of the Rotary Club Kyrenia'. I see ancient Turkish Cypriots, who look like ancient British people. Creased suits, sagging moustaches, sagging lips, watery eyes with sagging bags, some doddering, others limping, wrinkled hands on the silver knobs of elegant walking sticks. It's strange; as if Durrell's cabinet of frailties had come back to life, refreshed by an afternoon tea – thin cucumber sandwiches and club gossip.

I order myself a Brandy Sour; Niki only wants a mineral water.

'No Alexander?' I ask.

'I have to stop this endless remembering,' sighs Niki. 'Thank God my earlier life is not so far away from my life now, otherwise I'd feel as if I were watching a play in the theatre or looking over my own memoirs.'

She photographs the terrace, the swimming pool and the cement platform which juts a long way out into the sea. Finally we say our goodbyes. We will see each other again in Nicosia after my little trip.

There is a car hire place opposite the hotel. Oscar's. They only have jeeps or fully automatic Japanese cars. I settle on a Honda and fill in the form for four days' hire. I don't want to lose any time tomorrow morning.

Straight after breakfast I get behind the wheel and drive to Lapithos. I no longer recognise the road along the coast. It is, as far as the turning for Lapithos at any rate, entirely built up on both sides. Lapithos, by contrast, seems almost unaltered. The houses and their gardens sprawl over many levels. There are still destroyed and empty houses. The village seems as fundamentally precarious as it ever did: visiting it, you don't exactly know whether it is all about to be developed or disappear.

I come to the three-sided square where the Harrison House stands. They've prettied it up. What before was an expanse of cracked cement is now adorned with a green roundabout with a few trees in the middle of it. The trees encircle a memorial, a dark bronze bust of Atatürk on a granite pedestal. The whitewashed, somewhat offputting façade of the Harrison House on the street side is unchanged. The old, modest entrance is clearly no longer in use. At the end of the building there is now a huge entrance gate, preventing all access. Two security cameras are fixed above the gate. I knock. I lift up the heavy iron ring and bash it several times against the iron plate. I have composed in my head what I am going to say when someone opens up: that I lived here many, many years ago, spent two happy summers here and that I'd just like to cast an eye over the inner courtyard and the garden. No one comes. Nothing moves. I knock again, very loudly. No effect. I go to the house next door. An elderly woman is standing on her doorstep. She has heard the noise I've been making. She waves me in amicably. Now I tell her my story.

She introduces herself. She is the daughter of Orhan, who looked after the garden of the Harrison House back then.

'My father died a long time ago,' she says, 'but I can still remember your two girls well. They were so cheerful and they had perfectly blue eyes.'

She confirms Garo's story. The house belongs to Aşil Nadir. He has bought additional land around it and there is a big swimming pool now too.

'No, I can't let anyone in. I'm sorry. There are guards and they don't take a joke.'

'And Mr Nadir?' I ask.

'Mr Nadir is in London. A court case. We don't know when he'll be coming back.'

Why has this happened to me? I travel to my favourite house, to discover that it is closed up, inaccessible, and that in front of this barricaded building, which I cannot enter, they have erected an Atatürk! In my frustration I think of Lambousa. Perhaps there at least things have changed in my favour? I try several dead-end roads down to the sea, always in vain. I am about to give up the search, when behind a eucalyptus grove I spot a round, unrendered dome, which can only be part of a church. I take the next road, and am confronted with barracks and barbed wire, but there is a way leading alongside the fencing as far as an open field near to the sea. The 'built without hands' Acheiropoietos Monastery and the monastery church lie as before within the prohibited zone, but the church of Saint Evlavios rises up at the edge of the field, no fence or cordon, right in front of my nose. A young Turkish soldier runs up to me and asks me in immaculate English not to take photographs. A second soldier is standing in the field with a pickaxe in his hand.

'What's he doing?' I ask the soldier.

'Picking capers. The axe is for the snakes.'

'You speak such good English!'

'I live with my parents in London. All Turks have to complete their military service at a particular age, it doesn't matter where they live. It's dumped me here. I'm wasting my time.'

I wander once around the church. It is closed. Its shape reminds me of the Byzantine church in Kouklia, swathed in hemp ropes. There must have once been other buildings here, as shown by the meagre remnants of geometrical mosaics on the ground, the rhinestones and fragments of marble friezes. A mass of rock, covered in scrub, rises up conspicuously between the church and the fence of the prohibited zone. This bull-like block has been hollowed out, an apse cut into the rock, and there are niches, as in a Roman catacomb. This must be the chapel of Saint Evlavios. I can't quite take it in. How many fantasies, how much curiosity did I pour into visualising this chapel of rock, as I hunched over Rupert Gunnis's book at the Harrison House? And now I am standing in a gloomy vault with crudely hewn walls and animal dung in the corners, a space without mystery, stinking, bunker-like. I virtually have to say it out loud to myself: that that fabled trove of 6th-century silver was found here, the one with which the scholars of Byzantium set the world swooning. It makes me think of Ludwig Ross, the archaeologist who directed the excavations at Kouklia in 1888. He described his arrival at Kouklia, and the boundless disappointment that assailed him as he looked over that bald hill with its few, sad remains of the Sanctuary of Aphrodite, one of the mightiest temples of the ancient world. That is how I feel now.

I flee Lambousa, I flee Lapithos. Bellapais proves itself an effective antidote. My dejection melts away as I arrive in the heart of the village. It is untouched, unchanged. From the little table under the Tree of Idleness I look at the Abbey, the cypresses, which now soar above the cloister. I find Walnut Cottage and am delighted to discover that the two spacious houses on the other side of the ravine have been restored and are occupied again. I am pleased too that the lane leading to Lawrence Durrell's house has been renamed. It is now called *Acı Limonlar Sokak*. I wander happily up and down the old pathways and finally allow myself one more Brandy Sour in the Café of Idleness.

It's only late afternoon. I want to pay my respects to the Moon Beach, which we used to visit so often from Lapithos and then from Bellapais. My fear that it too will have been built over with drawing-board complexes and cheap, turn-key villas proves baseless. On a large sign at the end of the dirt track I read the reason why: 'Alagadi Turtle Beach.

In the months of June and July the beach is closed from 1900hr. Please watch out for the sea turtles!' A couple of sunshades are stuck in the sand and a few people are splashing about in the sea. I walk the length of the water's edge. Tiny, almost transparent crabs dart into tiny holes. At the sandstone hills which interrupt the bay I turn around, pull off my shirt and trousers and run into the water, still, in May, fairly cool. I lie on my back and stretch out my four limbs. The waves gently rock the dead man.

As I head back to the car I see a wooden hut in the dunes, on the left-hand side of the track, which I must have overlooked on my way in. It turns out to be an information centre for the 'Turtle Project'. A young English woman eagerly gives me the information: the project is run by Marine Biology students at the University of Exeter. She is just getting everything ready, because the nesting season begins in June.

'The sea turtles come at night. Most of them we already recognise. They only come when it's absolutely dark and quiet. Then they drag their insanely heavy shells up the beach, dig a deep hole and lay their eggs in it. We measure the tracks, the shells and the temperature in the holes and we scan the microchips in their shoulders. Last year the turtles dug one hundred and fifty holes. It's starting again soon.'

I think of Anna and Andrea. I gave them terribly false hopes in Lapithos. I didn't know that these animals only came onto the beach at night.

'And how long is it before the turtle babies hatch out?'

'After six or seven weeks they break open their shells,

scrabble their way to the surface and scull down towards the water, as quickly as they can. They have enemies, gulls especially, and foxes. At that age their shells are still very soft – later they become so hard that even sharks will break their teeth on them.'

In the night I dream of these animals, who have been paddling through the oceans for two hundred million years. But in my dream they are much smaller than in reality and they are playing with amphibians and lizards which look very much like geckos. I haven't yet seen a single gecko since my return.

The cult stone of Kouklia

I make my first stop at the highest point of the Troodos. From here the mountains, with their deep green pine forests and grey-white ribs of chalk, fall away on all sides to the sea. It is a clear day and I can make out the line of the coast. It is broken at one point by a large, bright expanse, flickering in the wind. That must be Limassol. Behind it the sea is shimmering.

I started out from Kyrenia early in the morning. My targets are Kouklia and Latsi. The border crossing in Metehan, a district in North Nicosia, was unproblematic. A few papers checked, the insurance, a stamp – that was it. No comparison with the extended procedures at the old GDR border, of which I am again reminded. I decided not to take the motorway via Limassol to Paphos, even though it would be much quicker, and instead to drive over the Troodos. I passed Kakopetria, Galata, Lagoudera, Platres and Pedoulas. I thought of the mighty calves of the Archangel Michael in the Church at Pedoulas, but I don't stop until this viewing spot. There is a well here, which Emin Çizenel would like. I hold my face under its cold stream, first the left cheek, then the right, then the mouth and chin. I eat a sesame whorl with some sour medlars I bought earlier in Kyrenia.

The Kykkos Monastery is my next stop. It has a long history.

An icon of the Virgin Mary the Compassionate – one of three said to have been painted by the Evangelist Luke himself and later given by the Byzantine emperor Alexius Comnenus to a Cypriot monk – is the miracle around which the monastery was built. First a chapel, then a church, then cloisters, then extension after extension. The newly erected buildings have repeatedly been swept away by fire, leaving only the holy icon, miraculously unharmed. You can't look at it. It's covered with a throw. There's probably just a singed, black wooden panel underneath, that's my theory.

Almost nothing you can see today is more than 150 years old. The monastery is not only the largest, it's also the most famous on the island. It has endless feudal landholdings and is, as a result, rich. It was also the favourite monastery of Archbishop Makarios, who came here many times and held overrunning masses. I wander through the halls, the two cloisters, and watch the monks and novices singing, but that sense of a mysterious secret, an unfathomable devotion, which assailed me in every one of the little barn churches, is absent.

Souvenir shops and snack bars are lined up, one after another, opposite the main entrance to the monastery. I walk up to one of the snack bars and order a couple of stuffed vine leaves and a glass of white wine.

'So, how do you like it here?' asks the sturdy stall operator.

I hesitate. I don't want to offend him and say that other, less dolled-up monasteries appeal to me far more.

'Aha,' he says, 'you like the nunneries? Is that it?'

No cleverer line occurs to me than: 'The mother of God here, painted by Saint Luke, outweighs all the nuns.'

He laughs good-humouredly and fetches me a few preserved fruits with a black, oozing walnut in the middle.

'Where are the other two icons the Evangelist painted?' I ask.

'One is in the Sumela Monastery on the Black Sea coast, near to Trabzon, and the other one is in the Megaspilion Monastery on the Peloponnese. But our icon is said to be the most beautiful by far. If we could only see it! My great grandmother actually touched it!'

As I am paying I notice that he safeguards his change in a dented tin saucepan. He rummages around in the pan, fishes out a five euro note, gives it to me and with a bright clink puts the lid back on his earnings.

The long, whimsical road down towards Polis is beautiful. After the pine forests come to an end, cypresses and red-flowering oleanders line the route, a long, unending driveway, but with no castle waiting for me at the end of it, only the sea. I bypass Polis, as even from a distance it seems frayed and unrewarding, and take the coastal road to Latsi. Even though I am expecting it, I am thunderstruck. That day-dreaming, tiny nowheresville, which consisted, as I've described, of three or four buildings, has become a boomtown. I cannot bear to think that the old Latsi, the deserted, ruled-by-nature Latsi, has been lost forever. I feel like an outsider or else an insider, but only within my own memories. The sea promenade leads past a vast marina. A wide phalanx of supermarkets, cafés and restaurants are spread out opposite the harbour. I am almost reassured when, in amongst all the concrete boxes and swarms of tourists, I spot Yiangos and Peter's old restaurant. It is jammed in between other eating places, but at least it is still there, and at least, as my waiter assures me, Yiangos is still around, old and frail, yes, but, unlike Peter, still amongst the living.

My route here from Kyrenia over the broad hilltops of the Troodos was long. It is already early evening. For ease, I take a modest room above the tavern, order some wine and to go with it, reviving an old, long-abandoned tradition, a plate of crabs in garlic sauce. A storm is approaching. Perhaps the last before the summer. I sit protected under the awning and watch the crazy theatre of the clouds, sweeping across the deep blue sky. At one point the sun finds a way through, then the rain falls again. Again the rainbows plunge into the sea. And then, in an instant, everything is calm. The wind abates, the clouds settle, the tourists fall quiet. It is the calm before the moon's grand entrance. It rises high above the horizon, a very large and very orange slice, so incandescent, so close, that it seems to bring disaster with it, and almost to make us afraid.

I leave the tavern and cross the coastal road. Leaving the nearest strip of shops behind me I take the first available dirt track inland and up a hill. I want to put the 'new' Latsi behind me, walk up onto the hill and fetch back into my memory the old, dreaming Latsi. I pass a row of apartments and I can't believe my eyes: it's the Elia Apartments, a relic of the old time. A shutter swings: in two rooms the lights are on, and on one balcony a naked young man is fiddling around. I keep walking into the scrubland and arrive on the top of a hill. The moon is smaller now, snow-white and silvery cold. For the whole night the sea will remain brighter than the land.

Next morning, at breakfast, the fishermen carry their catch past my table and on to the pick-ups waiting for them on the road. A squid writhes like a dark phosphorous marionette in a yellow nylon net. Mackerel spring and jerk in the plastic buckets, a living silver mass of hundreds upon hundreds of gasping gills and slapping fins. I walk one more time down onto the beach, to the left of the marina. Spiders' webs between the branches of a carob tree glisten in the morning haze. The sea is smooth and calm, as if sated and restrained by last evening's rain. With my back to the town I see only the sea and, at the end of the large bay, the foothills of the Troodos. That is my goodbye to Latsi.

In Paphos I meet no kings and no heroes, no goddesses and no pilgrims. The ancient city, already under the earth, has been buried a second time, smothered in a riot of mindless developments. I drive through bleak, unhappy modern shopping streets, searching for the access road to the motorway to Limassol. As the buildings finally begin to thin out, there are a few in-between landscapes and then once again 'Villas for Sale' and ugly abandoned construction sites. In the end I find the motorway and turn off at the level of Kouklia into the hinterland. The Château de Covocle, a Frankish castle, sits mightily on a hill. The Lusignans built it in the 13th century to guard over their sugar cane plantations. Above the central hall, held together by powerful Gothic buttressing, are the rooms of the new museum.

The only thing I want to see is the black cult stone, which I visited so often at the museum in Nicosia. It stands on a wooden pedestal. No ray of light strikes it, yet it gleams faintly. On ancient coins it is depicted under a tripartite canopy. Here every scrap of aura has been removed. It is unattractive. A plaque on the wall behind the stone informs me that Achaean settlers, finding the cult of the mother goddess Ishtar/Astarte already here, adopted the ritual worship of this conical, black stone. Ishtar becomes Aphrodite, the Greek goddess.

More than the stone, it is a sarcophagus from the 5th century before Christ that fascinates me now. It shows Polyphemus in delicate pastel shades and a gorgeous mix of styles, Greek and Oriental. He sits there, brown, hairy, hulking, a huge, blinded, giant bear. Next to him are three sheep in formation, trotting the length of the sarcophagus. Under the sheep's bellies, clinging to their bellies, I can make out Odysseus' companions, using this trick to steal out of the giant's cave. The cunning look in the three sheep's eyes is still following me, long after I have left the castle behind me.

East of the Sanctuary of Aphrodite, in a dip, stands the Katholiki church. Cords of strong hemp encircle the building all the way around. Apparently these cords ward off evil spirits and ensure that drought does not come to the area. The shadows of the cords show up so strongly against the outside wall of the round apse that it looks as if the apse wants to drag the entire nave behind it down the hill. The church was called Panagia Aphrodítissa as recently as two hundred years ago. Inside, I discover some frescoes on the western wall. Two masks spewing water personify the Euphrates and Tigris rivers. This arc back over a two-thousand-five-hundred-year stretch of time to the land of two rivers, to Mesopotamia, gives me a pleasant feeling of vertigo.

Through the railings protecting the archaeological excavations I see a group of women dressed in white, next to the south stoa. They are brandishing cymbals and tambourines. A woman in a long white tunic is swinging an incense burner. Is it a drama group? As I get nearer I hear that the women are speaking not Greek, but English. They are leaping about in a circle and bowing their torsos. 'Look at how classical we can be!' these esoterics seem to be saying, bathed in the midday floodlighting of Paphos – and are all the more ridiculous as a result.

I wander through Kouklia and settle myself into a bar on the village square. I have forgotten it is a Sunday. Now I hear a priest singing. Evidently his song is being broadcast outside over a loudspeaker. An Orthodox muezzin? The villagers couldn't care less and pick away at their *meze*. Later, when the song is over, the priest strolls across the square, an imposing, aloof authority in his long black caftan. He jumps into a pale blue Volvo and shoots off to the next village, the next little church. I copy him, drive down onto the motorway, via Pissouri and Limassol, and two hours later I am back in Nicosia.

Niki is out of town for two days. I can stay in her house with her two dogs and five cats. The Filipina maid opens up for me. She's just there to paint her nails for her Sunday outing. Her friend, a Bulgarian man, is looking at a Toshiba computer, absorbed in a virtual game. Then they go, though not before asking me whether I'd like to have some dumplings in sweet and sour sauce. I am finally alone. I swim in the pool, crossing the shadows cast onto the water by the tall fan palm. The dogs watch me paddling about. I tell them that I feel good, that I like the garden, the terrace with the jasmine bushes creeping up the wooden beams, the house, which harbours so many treasures, oil paintings of Levantine women, a bowl from İznik, an unusual tile from Isfahan decorated with a snake, dappled in many colours, books heaped on books and everywhere pictures by Niki, who is a bold colourist.

In the evening I walk out of Agios Dometios, the quarter where Niki's house is, and into the old city, to Ledra Street. Nicosia, the provincial city, reaches its most beautiful expression, it seems to me, on a Sunday. The suburbs are dead, but in the few shopping streets of the old city life is humming. I settle myself into a café and watch the parade. Hundreds of Asian women, who work in hotels or the houses of prosperous Cypriots, stroll up and down the street, dolled up, gentle and flirtatious. Were there not some young Greek couples, surrounded by swarms of children and with the women already pregnant again, were there not a few lost tourists, who really ought to be at the coast, were there not a few Russians and their molls, you might think you were in a district of Jakarta or Manila. Only the sandstone façades of the older buildings jar. I sense the debilitating boredom, which had already settled on the city 30 years ago. Everyone wants out, wants to flee to the coast or the valleys of the Troodos.

Later, on Niki's terrace, it is very quiet. A dog barks in the distance. A car door is slammed shut. A wind passes through the palms, becoming fiercer, so fierce that the noise of the fronds swept by the wind sounds like a body splashing into the water. Between the palms I can see the moon, on the wane, with a white aureole. The real, hot Cypriot summer is not yet here.

'What do you know about the difficulties of painting a glass?'

Aylin points to an armchair covered in a kelim and asks me to take a seat.

'A *çay*?' she asks. 'How lovely that you are visiting me, that you haven't forgotten me.'

Her studio near the *Büyük Han*, the great caravanserai, seems unchanged. Canvases on stretcher frames are leaned against the wall. A shaft of sun from the skylight falls on her easel and a work table piled with tubes and bowls. Bibelots of all kinds sit on a console by the wall, vases in the form of a bright pink hand, bowls with an Uzbek pattern, a little rag doll, a pair of yellowed photographs in thin brass frames.

Aylin is the most famous woman painter in Northern Cyprus. Denktaş once issued a stamp with her likeness on it. She is, I would say, already, at 65 years old, the doyenne of Turkish Cypriot artists. Her face is small and creased. Her black-rimmed glasses accent the severity of her face, a severity that dissipates the moment she speaks and fixes her green eyes upon you. A feeling of concentrated alertness runs through me, a feeling she has straightaway communicated to me. Even now she is watching me searchingly, as if she wants to grab a stick of charcoal immediately and sketch me.

'How long ago was it?' I murmur. 'Did I first visit you in

1985? I was enthralled by your pictures, so enthralled that I bought one instantly. An oil, which is hanging now in my house in Berlin. An unusual picture. In the foreground a checkered tablecloth, with a tulip-shaped glass on it, half full of dark brown tea, and behind it wooden bars, beams of wood one after another, leading down to the sea. A place for launching boats. Do you remember the picture? You said that it was the view from a teashop on the Bosphorus. The greenish yellow water, that's the Bosphorus.'

'Yes, I remember. A good picture. A peculiar perspective.'

'You weren't at all keen to sell it. You said to me: "What do you know about the difficulties of painting a glass?"'

The thought of Aylin came to me this morning, as I woke at Niki's house, perhaps because I was surrounded by so many pictures. I phoned her and she answered immediately, straightforwardly suggesting we meet around eleven at her studio. I fed the dogs, made myself a strong Nescafé and then walked to the pedestrian border crossing at the Ledra Palace Hotel. After the border post I turned right, crossed the city wall and arrived in the Arabahmet quarter. Here Nicosia ceases to be an indistinct city of diverse architectural styles. Here, in this quarter, it shows character. With funding from the EU and the UN, entire streets have been painstakingly restored. I gained a sense of how beautiful Nicosia within its Venetian city walls must have been right up into the thirties. The white-, blue- or orange-coloured plasterwork on the houses leaves the edges of the doors and windows free, so that the local golden sandstone can make an appearance. Almost all the houses have graceful porches and first-floor balconies bearing lattice-covered wooden kiosks, in which the women used to sit and watch the goings-on in the street below.

I oriented myself by the minarets of the Saint Sophia Cathedral, jutting out over the rooftops into the sky. I strolled past the gorgeous Dervish Pasha House and through the Basar district to the old caravanserai, which General Mustafa Pasha had had built in 1572, shortly after the Ottomans had conquered Cyprus. This *han* had also been lavishly restored. On the ground floor, where before there would have been stalls for mules and camels, there were now cafés, small galleries and shops selling embroidery and jewellery. Right beside it, in the Asmaaltı Sokak, a little before the Turkish baths, was the building where Aylin had her studio.

Now she is bringing in the tea with a plate of pistachio-filled *baklava*.

'I just bought these. I hope you like them.'

I look around the studio.

'Do you want to see a few pictures? You know that I'm a boring, figurative painter. Recently I've abandoned portraits and I've mostly been painting landscapes.'

She fetches her pictures one at a time out of the stack, rests them on the easel, waits a moment and then sets them against the opposite wall. There are sections of gardens, coastal landscapes, a lonely house with a lonely palm tree, the blue sequence of the Kyrenia Mountains.

'You're not boring,' I say. 'You couldn't be, not with your palette. There's no one else who puts colours together like you. It's completely unique. And another thing: you have a wonderful feeling for the earth, for the land. Not just running flat out to the horizon or to the sea, but also its arcs, its curves.'

'Really?' She chuckles quietly. 'Perhaps I'm not a boring painter, just a very slow one. We're already at the beginning of June and this year I've only managed five paintings that I'm really happy with. This one, for example.'

She gingerly places a new picture onto the easel. It is almost square, the colours are lustreless, almost dull. It's a view down over a fishing harbour from a raised position. Three boats are sitting in the pale grey water; their reflections in the water are dark green and violet. On the right is a truncated white wall and the sky over the horizon is white too, a grey white. A flight of steps leads down to a pontoon, which is suspended in a dull, lightless white. We never reach that distant place at the water's end, the painter seems to be saying, because it is inside us. She makes this feeling emerge out of the atmosphere in the picture, open and claustrophobic at once.

'I once asked you, how it is possible to paint a glass? Perhaps when I was beginning this picture, I asked myself: how can you paint a divided island? An island which is full of beauty, and yet where nothing has moved for fifty years? Perhaps I wanted to express my own weariness. Since the Annan Plan collapsed I've been feeling dull, exhausted, disaffected.'

'Let's carry on our conversation at Sabor,' I say. 'My treat?'

Aylin accepts: 'But we have to take a look at the *Bedestan* on the way there. It's the most daring building in the whole of Nicosia. The opposite of weariness. The epitome of elegance and energy.'

This *Bedestan* – which means something like covered market in Turkish – was in Byzantine times the Church of Saint Nicholas the Englishman. It stands right next to the Sophia Cathedral, now called the Selimiye Mosque. Apparently the Ottoman governors didn't see the need to change two churches into mosques, especially as the Sophia Cathedral was the biggest Gothic sacred building on the island, bigger even than the great cathedral of Famagusta. So they summarily declared the Church of Saint Nicholas to be a market hall. Later it served as a grain store for the whole city, then a market again, and by the end of the British colonial period it was pretty much neglected and gone to the dogs. Now this building too has been restored. The mix of Byzantine elements, Gothic additions and Venetian ornamentation combine in a joyous synthesis. The tall, slim columns, the five-sided apse in the choir, the marvellous portal, richly decorated with archivolts, together produce a 'heavenly striving', as Aylin attempted to encapsulate it.

'You start to have visions of life in the Middle Ages, don't you – with just a little bit of imagination. Don't you see those vain Lusignans on the royal gallery, swathed in brightly coloured brocade like parrots, and beneath those tricksters, the people paying homage to them?'

We have a great time at Sabor. We look out onto the choir of the cathedral and some Gothic buildings from the time of the Lusignans, with turquoise-painted shutters and solid-looking wooden balconies. For me it's as if the centre of the city takes shape from here outwards. The cold Villa Doluca tastes good. A cat stretches itself out in the deep shade.

Aylin picks up her thread from before: 'The collapse of Annan's peace plan has depressed me, it's true, even though I'm not very political. You know I was born in this district, and my parents and the bulk of my family. We aren't among the victims of the war and the division. None of us was forced to move. None of our goods and chattels was destroyed. When I was a child, there were the British. Then Cyprus became independent. Then there was Makarios, Clerides, Kyprianou and so on. The division of such a small island seems futile to me, and sad as well, and I've always thought that we will have to try to live together again. In a federation, with plenty of guarantees for us, the Turkish minority. Many of the artists here are of the same opinion.'

'I met Emin recently.'

'Well, Emin too. I like his stuff by the way. He belongs to another generation; he's a conceptual painter, always working in series, trying to demonstrate something to himself and to the world. But his well paintings are refreshing. They show skill. It's almost as if he lets us share in the moods and the feelings of the water.'

'Francis Bacon claimed that we are meat. Emin seems to claim that we are water.'

Aylin again chuckles her inimitable chuckle. We have one more *orta kahve* for the road. Then I walk back over the border. It's become hot. I am looking forward to Niki's terrace and the rustling and clattering of the palms, which this morning as I woke, seemed to have a regal air.

Famagusta, one more time

That evening Niki arrives back from Pomos, where she's been visiting her sister. In two days she's flying to London, having been invited to a conference to commemorate the hundredth birthday of Lawrence Durrell. She is rather frantic, as she still has to finish writing her paper. She has discovered a poem by Durrell, in some correspondence, – 'Not particularly good,' she says, 'but unknown and thus a scoop' – and is shining a light on some new aspects of his friendship with Alfred Perlès, who was a chum of Henry Miller as well.

'Two things,' she says. 'I'm going to dash off the paper this evening. Then – number one – I want to drive with you to Famagusta tomorrow and – number two – I want you to carry on staying in my house. You've got a whole week left in Cyprus. And I know you can write well here, much better than in some little hotel room. So carry on, as my guest.'

Next morning we make our way across the border at Agios Demetios and take the motorway towards Famagusta, at first through a sprawling industrial zone and then straight across the Mesaoria plain, which still retains the last shimmers of green. I was last in Famagusta 28 years ago. I'm excited, as I've always been fascinated by this city, with its medieval glory days and its decay. With Niki's assistance I recapitulate the facts one more time: Richard the

Lionheart conquered the island in 1191. He pursued the self-proclaimed ruler Isaac Comnenus, who retreated to Famagusta and then into the mountains of Kantara before Richard finally took him prisoner. Richard carried on to the Holy Land, where his friend Guy de Lusignan fought alongside him through the Third Crusade. Guy de Lusignan quickly lost his own Kingdom of Jerusalem to the Saracens. To thank him for his support, Richard the Lionheart offered him the island of Cyprus. Thereafter, for three hundred years, Famagusta under the Lusignans would become the new political and strategic arena for the West in the Eastern Mediterranean, a place of high finance and rich trade, later a bone of contention between Genoa and Venice before in the end came downfall after downfall, waves of destruction and unimaginable ruin.

'The distance between Venice and Famagusta,' says Niki, 'amounts to two thousand three hundred miles. France is further still. You have to imagine what that meant in the Middle Ages. Boat journeys lasting weeks, storms, pirates, trouble with shore leave, collisions. Aeroplanes have so radically changed our sense of time and space. We don't know what it means any more to ply the oceans, to negotiate a dangerous strait, to defy a storm.'

On the way into Famagusta, at the first roundabout, a gigantic Atatürk memorial awaits us. A tower of soldiers, paratroopers, mothers and farmers, to the greater glory of Turkey and the invasion of 1974.

'I'd like to become a terrorist and blow the whole thing into the sky.'

'Sit tight,' says Niki. 'Nothing has changed as much in the last twenty years as Famagusta's old city.'

She parks near the Church of Saint Peter and Saint Paul. In 1984–85, when I used to come here so often with the children and Karin, it was difficult to find a café of any sort or to track down a Coca-Cola for Anna and Andrea amongst all the ruined desolation. The area between the Provveditore's Palace and the Cathedral was a vast wasteland. Now a street runs right across it, a street that could as well be in Bodrum or Alicante. Souvenir shops, boutiques of counterfeit Hermès and Vuitton bags, quantities of trash and kitsch. Most gruesome of all is the *Türk Bankası*, a concrete bunker built right on the line of sight between the Governor's Palace and the Cathedral.

'Is it some special skill of the Turks, to spoil everything?' I murmur, crestfallen.

'Come on. Let's console ourselves at Petek,' says Niki.

Petek is a patisserie at the end of the street leading down from the Cathedral to the sea bastions. Less a patisserie than an overflowing emporium of all the sweet things in the world. The craziest cakes, cubes of blue, green, purple, red and yellow Turkish delight heaped up into castles and the boldest variations on *baklava*, *Şeker pare* and puff pastry rolls are laid out across over twenty metres of glass shelving, with an oriental instinct for decoration and glorious colour. How does this admirable instinct for presentation, for the nuances of colour and ornament, square with the brutalist block of cement up by the Cathedral? I can't get over it. I drown my grief in a grandiose mix of honey, sugar and almond paste.

Then we walk along the bastions, which number among the mightiest in the entire Mediterranean. They rise defiantly out of the overgrown rocks. Above the entrance to the old citadel the winged lion in white marble, corroded by sea salt, greets us as long ago. Why aren't plays performed here, with the fort as a backdrop, under this vast sky, the unrelenting light seeping into the Venetian courtyard in long, garish yellow threads? The backdrop at the Burgtheater in Vienna and Salzburg's Felsenreitschule have nothing to compare with this. As if to confirm it, a bird of prey lifts itself with loud wing beats and flies across to the St Nicholas Cathedral.

I especially want to see the Martinengo Bastion in the north of the old city. In my memory I still retain the image of three ruined churches in a no-man's-land, and for the first time since my return my remembered image does not turn out to be a delusion. The three churches are still standing there, lonely and apart, the Armenian Church, the Carmelite Church and the Church of Saint Anna. Spared the Turkish building developments, they offer a panorama of calm decay. Though gashed a thousand times, they have retained their form, they have their spirit. For me they encapsulate the Famagusta I saw so many years ago. I sit myself down on a stone ashlar and contemplate these Gothic buildings, robbed of all function, wrecked witnesses to an irretrievably lost time.

On the way back to the car Niki points out the twin churches of the Knights Templar and of St John, standing side by side, their outside walls perhaps no more than three metres apart, and then the Church of the Nestorians,

which served in Ottoman times as a cowshed. The Orthodox Christians adopted this church at the beginning of the
last century, Niki says, and dedicated it to Saint Georgios
Exorinos. For a long time it was the only church the Orthodox Christians used in the old city.

'For weddings especially, up until 1974,' Niki remarks.
'I remember it well, being in that church on Sundays as
a girl. Generally Greek life took place in Varosha, in the
new city, but the Orthodox wanted to have a foot in the
old city, which traditionally was the preserve of the Turkish
Cypriots.'

This Varosha, hermetically sealed since 1974, is of vast proportions – as I discover when Niki now drives us along the
length of its boundary. I had always thought Varosha consisted of a narrow strip along the sea's edge, those shattered
hotels and apartment blocks that you can see from the one
accessible point on the beach. But it is a huge area, which
stretches a long way inland and into which no person has
been for almost 40 years. It must be an El Dorado for biol-
ogists and zoologists. What kind of lizards, snakes, spiders
and rats have thrived here? How are the trees, bushes and
plants keeping, after four decades without cultivation,
without water, without pruning, without manure? Yet
again Uncle Mitsos's house comes into my mind, smothered in vine-like growths, the furniture split by damp,
the books crinkled and covered with a thick layer of sand
and dust.

'Uncle Mitsos is a good cue. There's another story I have
to tell you, but it's best suited to the place I want to drive

us to now. It's noon. We have to eat something. I know a seafood restaurant, a few kilometres past Salamis. We'll be there in half an hour.'

At Mardin Restoran the fish dishes come with the sounds of the sea included. The restaurant and its glazed terrace sit on a low hill by the sea. The restaurant is empty. We sit down at a table directly over the water, with a view of two, three mimosas, a jetty and a fishing boat bobbing aimlessly up and down. The dining room, almost a dining hall, is piled high with stuff, an old millstone, antediluvian harrows and amphorae encrusted with mussels. A stuffed swordfish dangles from the ceiling. Posters of Salamis and a few oil paintings hang on the walls. After we've selected two gilt-head sea bream in the kitchen, Niki tells her story.

'Uncle Mitsos wasn't just an obsessive bibliophile. He also spent his money on pictures by painters who he liked. George Pol Georghiou, for example, who lived in Famagusta and who he knew well, sold him a gorgeous female nude. And he bought a still life of melons on a plate and a scene of rural life on the Karpas peninsula from my mother, who was a distinguished painter. All of these pictures were hanging in the house in Varosha, which I've told you about many times already. Anyway, when Denktaş completely surprised everyone by opening the border, as you know I drove on the first day to Famagusta and then after that took a detour past Salamis before driving in an arc to Kyrenia via Lefkoniko. I stopped off at this restaurant. It was early afternoon, exactly like today, and I was not a little astounded. My mother's still life was hanging over the bar next to the till' – Niki gestures to show me the spot – 'and the village scene was hung there to the left of the toilets. I got entangled in a conversation with the owner of the restaurant. I told him that these pictures belonged to my family and that I wanted to have them back. The restaurant owner refused to give them up. He said they belonged to him now. They were the spoils of war. He used the Turkish word *ganimet*. A week later I drove back to this restaurant with two thousand pounds in my pocket. I showed the restaurateur the money and said I wanted to pay for the two pictures, even though by rights they belonged to me. I hoped that he might soften. But he only softened a little. He said that I could buy the picture of Karpas for this sum, but the other picture, the still life, he wouldn't be parted from.'

Our fish has arrived. I ask Niki whether the man who is busying himself behind the bar is the man in question.

'No. There was a change of ownership a couple of years ago. I don't know the new people. But back to my story. We argued. The man held firm and was only willing at most to give up one of the pictures. So, in an instant, while everyone was in the kitchen, I took photos of the still life. Then I went to see the best-known copyist in Nicosia, an old man called Andreas, who worked for the Archbishop's art collection and had produced copies of the most famous icons. I presented him with the photographs of the picture. I had discovered the exact dimensions as well, in a note-book, where my mother kept meticulous records of all her pictures. Andreas produced a perfect forgery. Then I went back to Mardin Restoran, not alone this time, but with three friends – and with the fake still life in the boot of my car. We carried out our plan. One friend engaged the cook in conversation in the kitchen; another friend had the restaurant owner show her a room, because there's a small hotel next door as well. The third wanted to know everything from the waiter about the spice garden, while I, as quickly as I could, switched the genuine picture for the dummy. I was extremely nervous. But it worked.'

'What an insane story! And you were so cool-headed! So where's the genuine still life now?'

'It's hanging at my friend Haris's, on loan.'

'And where's the forged picture?'

Already during Niki's story I have been scanning the walls of the restaurant. To the left of the toilets hangs a conventional landscape. But there's a load-bearing wall we can't see the other side of from our table, and the corridor into the hotel annex too. I jump up and Niki follows me. But the still life has vanished into thin air.

'I expect the last tenant took it with him,' Niki suggests. 'He was in love with those dripping dark red slices of melon on a yellow dish.'

There are sheets of glass on the tables in the restaurant. The owner, the former or the current one, has shoved photos between the glass and the tabletop, red-tinged snapshots of family celebrations, of guests, local celebrities perhaps, and of the restaurant itself. We go from table to table examining the photos pressed under the glass. Suddenly it is as if Niki has been electrocuted. Very clearly, in a Polaroid of the back wall of the local bar, you can make out the still life, in a dark wooden frame. I lift up the sheet of glass, fish out the photo and slip it to Niki. She spirits it away into her wallet.

'Thank you,' she says. 'Everything must be documented.'

I have seen no more geckos

The unfamiliar is much more exciting than the familiar. After a quarter of a century, so much of Cyprus is no longer familiar to me. The island has changed and I can scarcely make it and my memories coincide. My memories are sharp and free, I believe, of false emotions or that fatal longing to see things as I left them. My feelings are not so important. There's no question that the opening up of the border is the biggest of all the changes. Yet strangely the Cypriots have not grown more hopeful as a result. It is rather as if the open border has taught the Greek Cypriots that they ought to concentrate on their part of the island. Their former properties, once they could see them again with their own eyes, proved to be out of reach. What a paradox. I have no property here. But the beach below Lapithos, where so many times we bathed and enjoyed ourselves, no longer exists. In its place are 64 beachfront 'units', which a large billboard advertises from 34,800 Turkish lira each. Thus for around 15,000 euros you can acquire a concrete box in the midst of other concrete boxes. In this way Paphos has been devastated, Latsi built over. Glyn Hughes is old and ill. George Lanitis is dead, Lionel Miskin is dead. The house in Lapithos, Sir Austen Harrison's gorgeous summer house, is inaccessible, in the hands of a crook. I have seen no more geckos. They are not DDT resistant. But under the Tree of Idleness I did hear Uzun's saying: 'He has the will to live of half a lizard.' He meant the old café owner, who brought me strong Brandy Sours.

And, equally strangely, a great deal remains untouched. The villages of the Troodos, the little churches with the beguiling glory of their frescoes. The Archangel Michael's calves are as thick and powerful as 28 years ago, as a thousand years ago. The Karpas peninsula has remained archaic. For how much longer? Get past the business parks and the new-build developments, push on into the heart of the old cities, and things are as they were. The time between then and now is abolished. The alleys and squares around the Abbey of Bellapais, the inner harbour of Kyrenia in the midday stillness bewitch as they ever did. The three brown Gothic churches next to the Martinengo Bastion in Famagusta bear witness to the splendid Frankish Middle Ages, as they ever did.

I pass these last days in Nicosia in glorious solitude. Niki is in London. Horst in Düsseldorf. Arianna with her mother in Paphos. Emin in Istanbul. Garo I don't know where. I write. I stroll over the border into the northern part of the city and treat myself at Sabor. I visit Aylin for a cup of sweet tea with pine nuts. I drop in at Moufflon, the bookshop. Ruth, the taciturn, softly spoken Armenian, is holding the fort, surrounded by precarious towers of books. I buy a thick book of pictures. It's called *Cyprus Remembered* and contains several hundred photos by Reno Wideson, a Cypriot born in Larnaka in 1920, who was called Evryiades and then changed his name when he went to England. Later he worked under Lawrence Durrell in the press office of the colonial government. Most of these black-and-white photos were taken between 1950 and 1960. Together they constitute a stratum of time before 'my' Cypriot time in the middle of the eighties. They record an overwhelmingly rural, sleepy Cyprus, which was already scarcely there in 1985 and today no longer exists at all. The rhythm of island life depicted in these very frank photographs is so different from the rhythm of the island today. I look over these pictures again and again and I note how violently and radically life on Cyprus has changed, in a relatively short period of time. The shadows of palms move across the paper on which I am writing these final lines. In a photograph by Reno Wideson an old fisherman from Kyrenia is looking at me. It's a half-length portrait. He is heavily wrinkled around the eyes, truthful eyes, squinting against the sun, with wrinkles on his forehead, stubble, a threadbare jacket. He is smiling. It's a very guarded smile, and I know why.

Three Poems by Niki Marangou

Street Map of Nicosia

Looking at the street map
of Nicosia and its suburbs,
Fuad Pasha Street ends on Dionysou and Herakleitou
Defne Yüksel on Hermes Street
Yenidze Şafak on Leontiou Mahaira
right nearby to the Rocca Bastion.
On old maps the river runs through the middle of the city
but Savorniano, the Venetian, changed its course
to fill the moat with water.
There on Sundays the housemaids
from Sri Lanka spread out their shawls
and eat together.
The palm trees remind them of home.

For my friends in the North
Because I talk of roses,
of the diffusion of light,
of the helplessness of love,
and of our fleeting life,
don't think, friends in the north,
that what happened in '74
doesn't spread like a stain on my life,
day after day.

The moon rises out of the sea
like a slice of watermelon,
and my dead mother on the veranda
of our home in Famagusta is calling us
to come out of the water.
The other day, on the wall of a taverna on the Karpas,
I saw a picture she had painted. A taverna
made of stolen chairs, stolen tablecloths,
stolen doors, stolen handles.
'It's my mother's,' I told the owner.
'Her name is written here.'
'But now it's mine,' said the man,
who came from a land where the sun rises
(that's how his wife described him to me).
'It's mine now,' he said, *ganimet*,*
that what they call it in Turkish.

Istanbul, October 2005

---

*Turkish for 'loot'

Letter to Dionysis
We cannot speak with certainty
of kingfishers or nightingales

Lucian

You know, Dionysis,
it's not easy for us nowadays to talk
with certainty about kingfishers or nightingales
because we haven't lived in houses
where cocks were sacrificed on the foundations
because we haven't slept on mattresses
with crosses embroidered on the four corners
where coins fell
of gold and silver
and seeds of cotton and sesame

because we haven't streamed out
onto the streets late at night
to the brightly lit houses
with Lazaruses swathed in yellow flowers
their blossom-strewn beds decked
with garlands and grains
birds lizards leaves
flour fennel candles and honey
softer than sleep

and so, Dionysis,
in the midst of the 'general confusion

of the imprecision of feelings'
as I'm drinking a coffee
on a Friday morning
I want simply to say
that I've missed you very much.

Three poems by Joachim Sartorius

The cult stone of Kouklia

It's a meteorite.
A lump of stone, whose fire
went out on impact. Its thin
glassy smelted crust recalls
that meeting
of sky and earth,
it lures searchers.

It's unattractive, grey-green
not black, the cone-shape
not regular, an idol
that doesn't rhyme
with the beauty-shaped,
Foam-birthed.
It will be the secret
of the pilgrimage.

The tall, self-sufficient
columns, crowned with a double horn,
can be seen on coins.
The pure flame, rising
into the sky, we must imagine.
We wander round the glass case.
In front of the museum trucks
laden with ancient marble thunder
over the streets of memory.
The stone cannot be touched,
not be kissed.

Agios Kassianos in Nicosia

From the window a view of a minaret, which means cross
and comes from Mişr, Egypt. At night it has
a wreath of green neon tubes around its thick neck.
At night the stink of the Pakistani bush comes from the
    garden.
Below, on the blocked street, at night, Greek soldiers
curse the Turkish soldiers by the sandbags.
Houses blown up: time stopped. No youth anywhere.
The cats make the two Lefkosias into one land.

From the balustrade
fatty locusts fall into their pointed mouths.
They sharpen and sharpen their claws in the sand.
Heaps of sand, heaps of cells. It's just good there are
friendly hands to close your eyes, eyes which beg
for no reason that the shell will not be too hard.

(And if you stretch out to pick the pomegranate,
then you have to come to this place again and again,
this place near Famagusta, Lapta, Lefkosia, heavy yellow.)

At Paphos Harbour

What does the gulls' breath smell of?
Shells? Seaweed?
Flat fish with brown skin?
They sit, irises of pierced white,
on small, limp, blue waves
and gaze into the expanse –

the evening a sudden pink
and the land of sleep from East to West.

The old men on the bench,
hard knots, loosen themselves,
remember how mild it was
swimming in her.

The street glistens down to the harbour.
Its spine uncoils direct from the sun,
which sets, hissing (the prophets, the gulls).

Back then we took Paphos for a god.
His big toe, it was said, reached the treeline
of the Troodos. But now it is a futile town

(only sometimes remembered still
like a palace fire).

Acknowledgements

To all the friends who helped me with advice and tips, a big thank you. In particular, thank you to Horst Weierstall, Arianna Economou and Lellos Demetriades.

From all who appear in this book, I ask for their forbearance, as I have made my own portraits from them and in the process transformed them into literary characters.

Most of all, thank you to Niki Marangou. Without her this would have been a different and a poorer book and without her hospitality I would still not have finished it.

She was looking forward to this book, which she had read in proof. A few weeks before it was first published she died entirely unexpectedly and in tragic circumstances, in a car accident in the Egyptian desert. So this book has become as well something it was never meant to be, an epitaph.

March 2013
Nicosia and Berlin

A note on place names

For towns and villages I overwhelmingly use the Greek, not Turkish names: Kyrenia not Girne, Lapithos not Lapta and so on. When I began writing I had to decide because I could not in my book use both names with a slash – as is usual in contemporary maps. Since I lived from 1984 to 1986 in the capital of Cyprus, in Nicosia, in the Greek part, and more or less exclusively heard the Greek names even for places in the Turkish-occupied North, I decided to follow what I heard then, my memory.

Selected reading

Anderson, Perry: *The New Old World*. London 2011

Balfour, Patrick: *The Orphaned Realm. Journeys in Cyprus.* London 1951

Cesnola, Luigi Palma di: *Cyprus, its Ancient Cities, Tombs and Temples*. London 1877

Chotzakoglu, Charalampos: *Religious Monuments in Turkish-occupied Cyprus*. Nicosia 2008

Delaval Cobham, Claude: *Excerpta Cypria – Materials for a History of Cyprus*. New York 1969

Durrell, Lawrence: *Bitter Lemons*. London 1957

Frazer, James George: *The Golden Bough*. New York 1974

Gunnis, Rupert: *Historic Cyprus*. London 1936

Hunt, David: *Footprints in Cyprus. An Illustrated History.* London 1982

Kouyialis, Theoklis: *27 Centuries of Cypriot Poetry. An Anthology*. Nicosia 1983

Liebe, Klaus: *Zypern*. With photographs by Gerhard P. Müller. Munich und Lucerne 1984

Ludwig Salvator, Archduke of Austria: *Levkosia – die Hauptstadt Zyperns*. London 1983

Luke, Sir Harry: *Cyprus under the Turks 1571–1878*. Oxford 1921

Marangou, Niki: *From Famagusta to Vienna*. London 2010

Marangou, Niki: *Selections from the Divan. Poems.* Translated and introduced by Stephanos Stephanides. Nicosia 2001

Montis, Costas: *Moments. Poems.* Translated by Amaranth Sitas and Charles Dodd. Nicosia 1965

Porcacchi, Thomaso: *L'Isole piu famose del mondo.* Venice 1572

Rimbaud, Arthur: *Complete Works, Selected Letters, A Bilingual Edition.* Translated and edited by Wallace Fowlie, revised by Seth Whidden. Chicago and London 2005

Seferis, George: *Collected Poems.* Expanded Edition. Translated, edited and introduced by Edmund Keeley and Philip Sherrard. Princeton 1981/London 1982

Seferis, Giorgos: *Ionische Reise.* Translated into German from the Modern Greek by Gerhard Emrich. Frankfurt am Main 2006

Thubron, Colin: *Journey into Cyprus.* London 1975

Wideson, Reno: *Cyprus Remembered.* London 2010

Zeilinger, Johannes (ed): *Cypern, Orient und Okzident. Ein Lesebuch.* Munich 1997